SHOULD

How Habits of Language
Shape Our Lives

Rebecca Smith

Beaver's Pond Press, Inc.
Edina, Minnesota

ISBN 1-931646-85-6

Library of Congress Catalog Number: 2003113721

Book design and typesetting: Mori Studio
Cover design: Mori Studio
Cover photo: Virginia Campbell.

Printed in the United States of America

First Printing: November 2003

06 05 04 03   6 5 4 3 2 1

Beaver's Pond Press, Inc.

7104 Ohms Lane, Suite 216
Edina, MN 55439
(952) 829-8818
www.BeaversPondPress.com

To order, visit www.SHOULDbook.com or www.BookHouseFulfillment.com or call 1-800-901-3480. Reseller and special sales discounts available.

To Ella,
who makes everything better.

We speak.
And what happens?
We inform, we connect, we confuse, we console,
we enlighten, we enrage, we deceive, we defend,
we promise, we ponder.
We write—perhaps more carefully than we speak—
but with the same result.
This is the nature of language.
However careful we are to be clear,
language remains as powerful,
as beautiful, as devastating,
and as mysterious as
a kiss.

Table of Contents

Introduction
Shoulds and *Oughts* and *Can'ts*

I was itchy. 2001 had a bumpy finish, and it left me uncomfortable in my skin. I wanted to feel new, so in January I took a personal development course—something I'd never done before. I wanted answers.

At the end of the second day, we did a goal-setting exercise. I'd spent much of the previous year developing a retail web site in hopes of becoming the first internationally trusted fashion authority in the impersonal world of e-commerce. While I was certain that my goal-setting exercise would help me clarify how best to advance my current project, it didn't.

I'd hoped for a modicum of celebrity from my role as on-line fashion authority, and I had planned to use that celebrity to find opportunities for public speaking. When I did my goal-setting exercise, I discovered that I didn't want to be an on-line fashion authority; I wanted to be a public speaker.

The following month I took another section of the same course. In it we did a group exercise to discover what external forces get in the way of our accomplishments. The group generated answers like fear, anxiety, and misplaced priorities. Then someone said, *"shoulds* and *oughts* and *can'ts."*

In the weeks that followed, the significance of *shoulds* and *oughts* and *can'ts* sunk in. I realized that most of my own choices were made with an overriding sense of obligation. And I noticed that my language consistently reflected the oppression of that obligation. With a vocabulary weighted with *shoulds* and *oughts* and *can'ts*, I sounded bound. I reasoned that if my experience of oppression was so thoroughly influencing my language, maybe I could alter my language to lessen my experience of oppression.

Shoulds and *oughts* and *can'ts* quickly grew into eight words and phrases. They are the language of oppression.

should　⌒　*have to*　⌒　*must*　⌒　*ought to*

try　⌒　*need*

can't　⌒　*have no choice*

My next step was to eliminate this language from my vocabulary. I avoided the eight words and phrases, often fumbling for what to say instead. As I noticed how often these words came to mind, I realized how much oppression they'd created for me throughout my life. I'd felt obligation in every task I *had to* do. I'd felt the frustration of striving every time I *tried*. I'd felt restricted every time I *had no choice*.

And not long after taking on the elimination of these eight words and phrases, I noticed what happened when they were gone. When I stopped telling myself what I *should* do, I began asking myself what I *desired* to do. I began doing everyday tasks that I'd always done with a sense of obligation (I *should* run to the mail box; I *have to* grab my bag) as indulgences of my desire (I'd *like to* run to the mail box; I *want to* grab my bag).

Once I stopped assuming oppression, I saw my choices. I realized that I choose my tasks every day. I choose how I approach those tasks. I choose what I see in them and how I experience them. I realized that self-oppression is a choice too, and that I no longer wished to choose it.

SHOULD is the study of how the language of obligation, frustration, and restriction creates oppression in our lives. *SHOULD* presents solutions to the problems we create with our habitual use of this language, and it explores what happens when we eliminate it. Once we stop listening to our *should*-sayers, once we stop being *should*-sayers ourselves, and once we learn to refer to ourselves with reverence, we reclaim *Self*.

I believe that personal dissatisfaction is caused by a failure to honor our*selves*. If we fill our lives with obligation we act in response to a sense of duty—not to our own desires. If we fill our lives with frustration we act in desperation—not confidence. And if we fill our lives with restriction we act in opposition—not in pursuit of what we desire.

Careful readers of *SHOULD* will change how they view the world, how they view other people, and most importantly, how they view them*selves*. If you feel obligated, it will point you back to your desires. If you feel frustrated, it will show you your competence. And if you feel restricted, *SHOULD* will open you to your own unlimited possibilities.

Read *SHOULD* with a critical mind. Run its ideas through your own experience. Discover for yourself what you've been creating with your words, and decide what you'd like to create from now on.

You will see yourself in this book.

Self-Portrait

Let's paint a self-portrait. It doesn't matter how much artistic ability you have; it's an imaginary painting.

First familiarize yourself with your materials. Picture a canvas any shape and size along side a palette of oil paints in any colors you desire. Oil paints are dense in feel and rich in color. As oil paint touches a fresh canvas it goes on smoothly. Big brushes drenched in paint make brilliant swaths of color; small brushes make fine details. Oil paint stays wet for days, smears when you run its colors together, and marks (often permanently) everything it touches. While real oil paintings can take days, weeks, even months to complete, imaginary oil paintings can be completed in a matter of minutes.

Now we'll paint. Start with a figure to represent you. You may imagine a perfect likeness, a purely abstract representation, or anything in between. Now add symbols anywhere on the canvas that have meant something to you in the past—perhaps religious symbols or something representing family, old friends or your past interests. Now paint your past sorrows and joys.

In the next phase of your self-portrait, paint over the old symbols that no longer represent you with new symbols that do. If your old symbols still represent you, embellish them with contrasting or complementary colors. Paint over your past sorrows and joys with an updated set. Add colors that have meaning for you. But notice as you add more color that the paints don't go on as cleanly as they did when you started. At this point there are so many layers of wet paint on your canvas that what you may intend as red gets muddied to brown. Add more symbols and colors to your painting for as long as you wish.

When your canvas is full of paint and the colors and images have thoroughly blurred into one another, step back and look at what you've got. Your combination of images—your crowded concoction of colors and textures—is a picture of what this book will refer to as the *pseudo-self*. It's *You*, essentially, but it's *You* buried beneath many layers of identity.

Now pick up a paint scraper and gently scrape the paint off. Your oils have remained as wet as when you first applied them, and your canvas is easily scraped to its original smoothness.

What remains of your self-portrait is an after-image that retains traces of all of the images you've put onto it. Your portrait is at once *all images* and *all images removed*. What you have made is a portrait of the Self.

For the purposes of this book, the Self is *You* in your purest, least affected form. That Self is a combination of the pure original canvas beneath, and the indelible (and often beautiful) imprint of identity. This working definition of the Self—a *You* as true and bare and unaffected as possible—will function as the center-point for many of the concepts in *SHOULD*.

The Layers

You began life as a clean canvas. In your self-portrait, the thick and muddied layers of paint represent all of the elements of identity that you have taken on until now. It is likely that you have layers of identity that you have taken on deliberately; you may consciously identify yourself by your temperament, your cultural heritage, your political or religious leanings, or by a physical characteristic. But you began painting your self-portrait in infancy, so it is inevitable that you have also taken on layers of identity unconsciously.

Everyone and everything that penetrates our senses—family, friends, teachers, acquaintances, TV, movies, music, books, magazines, and advertising—influences us. And most of these influences, at some point or another, tell us what to do. We internalize these influences, and over time we learn to use their voice to tell ourselves what to do. These internalized influences comprise the *voice of Other*. The voice of Other has been with most of us for so long that we have lost our ability to distinguish that voice from our own. But *I should, I have to, I must, I ought to, I need, I try, I can't,* and *I have no choice* are all the voice of Other. Every time we use this language we speak to ourselves with a voice other than our own.

When you tell yourself what you *should, have to, must,* or *ought to* do, you put on a layer of obligation, and identify yourself as oppressed. When you tell yourself that you *need* something or that you are *trying,* you put on a layer of frustration, and identify yourself as oppressed. When you tell yourself that you *can't* or you *have no choice,* you put on a layer of restriction, and again, you identify yourself as oppressed. The voice of self-oppression is the voice of Other; it is not your *own* voice.

Eliminating the language of self-oppression from your vocabulary prevents you from taking on new layers of obligation, frustration, and restriction. Using self-empowering language in its place—using words that convey your own desire, competence, and ability—scrapes away old layers of obligation, frustration, and restriction. The more layers you scrape away, the closer you get to the smooth canvas with only a shadow of identity upon it, and the more authentic you are. The closer you get to being who you truly are, the greater possibility you have for living a life that satisfies you to the core.

In our painting metaphor, this book is your box of scrapers. While the tools in it will not help you remove *all* of your layers (there's no sandblaster in this box) they will increase your awareness of the layers you have. They will show you the experience your layers create for you. And they will teach you how to remove as many layers as is possible for you. It is up to you whether you put the practices in this book to use. A scraper only works if you use it.

As its title suggests, this book's focus is language. Language is a portal into the inner workings of our relationship with ourselves, and there is a lot we can do with language to tinker with that relationship.

Since our working definition of Self is a canvas marked with the imprint of identity, it follows that we can repaint ourselves. A painter can continue to create on a canvas indefinitely. And with a process that involves applying and scraping layers of paint, a painter can change an imprint almost completely. What may begin as a dark and muddied mess can emerge as a dazzling portrait of the sun.

PART ONE

Creation

"In the beginning was the Word."
—the New Testament

Chapter One

Creating by Habit

People create. We create gadgets, technologies, cities, and children. We create connection, opposition, and action; information, inspiration, and language. And we use our creations to create more things.

We create with language. We create songs and stories—poems, philosophies, religions, and lies. We create discord with cruelty and comfort with kindness. Decisions are made with language—as are promises, apologies, threats, war declarations, and peace accords.

We have a profound ability to influence each other with language. Our ability to influence ourselves with language is even greater.

Our Language Creates Our Experience

While pure experience *can* exist without language, we rarely keep language at bay long enough to experience anything in its purity. Occasionally something happens that takes our breath away. Say you are hiking and suddenly you see an eagle take flight. If that moment is stunning enough to impede your ability to speak or even think, you may experience that moment without language. In that rare instance, language does not shape your experience. But as soon as you regain your ability to think and speak, you begin to write the history of that stunning moment. Perhaps you tell yourself how amazing it is that such a large bird moves so gracefully, or you recall that you weren't sure it was an eagle until it landed. Once you add language to your stunning moment, it no longer exists as pure experience. You *recreate* your experiences with the stories you tell yourself about them.

In most instances you tell yourself stories about what you do as you do it. If you plant a garden, you may tell yourself that you enjoy gardening or that your garden looks better than it did last year. Whether these thoughts are articulated or not, they make up the stories that shape your experiences. For most of us, the stories we tell ourselves about what we do are not deliberate. It may never occur to us that we could tell ourselves better stories to improve our experiences.

Our daily stories are shaped by habit. If your habits of language include words that convey self-oppression, you increase your feelings of oppression by habitually telling yourself that you are oppressed. Your time in the garden may be shaped by the language of obligation, restriction, or frustration; perhaps you *have to* get your plants in today because you *can't* tomorrow, and you *need* to get them planted before they die. If you allow oppressive stories to shape your everyday experiences, you will experience oppression every day.

By the time we reach adulthood we may have acquired thousands of deeply ingrained habits of language. But these habits are not the product of our thoughtful consideration of how we desire to speak. It is far more likely that our current set of verbal habits is, at least in part, a collection of ticks and ruts adopted without consciousness. Once our linguistic habits are in place, we create with the momentum of those habits.

Our Language Creates Our Picture of Self

Our self-oppressing language creates a picture of an oppressed Self. If your language implies that you are pressured by obligations *(I should, I have to, I must, I ought to)*, that you are frustrated *(I need, I'm trying)*, or that you are restricted *(I can't, I have no choice)*, you expose your daily experience of oppression. But your self-oppressing speech may not be limited to words that convey obligation, frustration, and restriction. If you hide behind assertions of what's *right, appropriate,* or *proper*, you rely on ethics rather than your own values. This reliance on ethics creates a picture of you as someone not capable of making good decisions on your own. And if you admire self-discipline and self-restraint but sneer at self-celebration and self-promotion, you reveal your suspicion of the Self. Everything you accomplish starts with you. If you picture yourself as oppressed, deferential, and untrustworthy, you have your work cut out for you.

But just as the artist who paints, scrapes, and paints more is free to create and recreate a painting, so are you free to paint and repaint your picture of Self. Trading self-oppressing language for self-empowering language can be as transformative as scraping off a patch of mouse-gray and replacing it with canary-yellow. Everything you think and say about yourself creates your picture of Self. Most of us create that picture unconsciously, leaving to mere habit what may be one of the most meaningful tasks we have.

Our Language Creates Our Reliance on Self – or Other

Consider what you know about responsibility. As a child you were introduced to responsibility as blame. You learned to equate "I am responsible for all that I do" with "I am to blame for all that I do wrong." Later, but also as a child, you learned about being a "responsible person"—or a model citizen. This understanding of responsibility taught you that you are responsible to uphold an ethical standard of propriety. While ethical responsibility has its merits, there is great distance between this early sense of responsibility as an obligation to be "good," and a maturely held sense of *personal* responsibility. When you are *personally* responsible, you do not rely on your interpretation of ethical values; you rely on your *own* values.

French philosopher Michel Foucault wrote that liberty is a practice, not a condition, meaning we're free only to the extent to which we practice our freedom. Responsibility works the same way: we are responsible only to the extent that we practice responsibility. But *personal* responsibility goes one step further. We are *personally* responsible only to the extent to which we *personalize* our responsibility.

Personalizing responsibility is a way to practice self-reliance. When your every decision is based on your own values and you access those values through your own desires, you rely on your*self*. If you lack a fundamental trust in your own virtue, however, you doubt that your values will lead you to "right" action. And that lack of trust in your values sends you looking elsewhere for guidance. Every voice that comes from outside of you—every voice that does not report your own values and desires—is the voice of Other. The voice of Other reports what your family, culture, and religion deem appropriate. It tells you what's ethical and right, but it does not tell you anything about your*self*.

Notice in the examples that follow, how ethical responsibility evolves into personal responsibility, and how our language reflects that evolution:

Say for example, you have an opportunity to be of service to a charitable organization. With a sense of ethical responsibility you might tell yourself ◡

◡ I *should* do this.

With "I *should* do this," you imply that you intend to take action because it is the correct thing to do. With *I should*, you may or may not act according to your own values as you summon instead the values of your internalized voices—voices that reflect your interpretation of societal values and ethical standards. *Should* is the voice of Other, and your reliance on it prevents you from being personally responsible for any decision it compels you to make.

You may take several steps toward personal responsibility before actually getting anywhere near it, as in ◡

◡ It's *right* to do this.

You depend on your notion of what's *right* to keep you out of trouble. Instead of considering your own values, you look to Other for its reading of ethical and societal norms. When you assert the objective rightness of your *personal* decisions, you rely on Other rather than yourself to decide.

You may use more personal language without actually personalizing your responsibility at all, as in ⌣

⌣ It's right for *me* to do this.

This seems to move you closer to acting from your own values, but your lingering deference to what's *right* is impersonal. In practice, an impersonal sense of what's right can make for a helpful point of departure. But few of us depart from it. We act on obligation to an ethical sense of right, rather than trusting in our own values. This example teases with its promise of self-reliance, but in the end it delivers only a reliance on Other.

You do not fully personalize your responsibility until you come to ⌣

⌣ This is what *I* desire to do.

An expression of your own desire is an expression of Self, and the act of following your own desire is an act of self-reliance. With no sense of obligation to convention—with no nod to ethical standards—you take full responsibility *as you act.*

The evolution from responsibility-as-blame to ethical responsibility and finally to personal responsibility is the evolution from creating by habit to creating deliberately.

Our Language Creates Personal Satisfaction–or Not

Personal satisfaction is satisfaction of the Self.

Just as responsibility is made personal by your deliberate personalization of it, so is satisfaction made personal by deliberate personalization. It is only when your purpose is rooted in your own desires, that you will find personal satisfaction in fulfilling your purpose.

Accidents

The power of language is not diminished by your lack of attention to it. If you are careless with your language it creates just as powerfully as if you'd chosen your words with perfect deliberateness. The language of your unconscious thoughts, of your over-rehearsed speeches, of the songs that get stuck in your head, the language of your criticisms and your complaints, of your questions and your answers creates constantly.

Language creates.
Whether you want it to or not.

PART TWO

Word Problems

"Watch your own speech, and notice
how it is guided by your less conscious purposes."
–George Eliot

CHAPTER TWO

Creating Obligation:
Should, Have to, Must & Ought to

Feeling obligated is not the same as *being* obligated; sometimes they bear no resemblance to each other. Say you are one of two adult children of frail, aging parents. When close family members appear to be in *need*, you may conclude that you are obligated to help them. But if you are the child making all of the visits, cooking, cleaning, and accompanying parents on outings, you may do it all out of love, with no *feeling* of obligation at all. If you are the other sibling—the one who does nothing to help—you appear to be free from obligation. But your guilt over not helping may ensure that you still *feel* the burden of the dozens of obligations you make no effort to meet. Obligation is a concept and we are free to experience it—or not.

Our common understanding of obligation is that it requires something of us. We think each obligation requires our action, or at minimum our attention. If we fail to give it that action or attention, we fail to fulfill our obligation. While we are likely to experience that failure as a personal failure, we can trace it back to a wholly impersonal source: the voice of Other. Even though we most often say *I should*, *I have to*, *I must*, and *I ought to*—and even though we say them to declare what are presumably our *own* intentions—they're impersonal.

The language of obligation binds us to our tasks—*I must* remember to pick up some bread on my way home. It shapes our to-do lists—*I have to* get my bills paid by Monday. It reports our conscience—*I should* stop picking fights with my brother. But as personal as any of these statements sounds, none of them reports a desire of the Self. In practice, we can remember to pick up bread because we *want to*, we can pay our bills on time because it *feels better* to pay them on time than it does to pay them late, and we can stop picking fights because we *value* our relationships. This latter group of intentions and the actions that follow them are based on desires of the Self.

For most of us, trusting obligation to guide us feels much safer than trusting ourselves. But all language creates. If you use language that implies obligation, you create the burden of obligation for yourself and others every time you use it.

Other-Reliance

⌒ *Should I?*

⌒ Maybe *I should.*

I should is a self-contradiction. It begins with *I*, an indisputably personal reference, but it concludes with an assertion of obligation to Other. It undermines its intention by splitting its focus.

The phrase *I should* is often used in decision-making, creating confusion for us from the outset. If you figure out what you *should* do, you concern yourself with what's *right* by some external standard. When your decisions are based on *shoulds* and *shouldn'ts*, you are not the source of your decisions.

Without Self as source, there is no self-reliance. Under the influence of its opposite, other-reliance, you look outside of yourself for guidance. Under other-reliance you may fret about what your family, religion, or culture might consider appropriate instead of peacefully acting on your own values. If you are locked in other-reliance, you are always careful to do what you *should*—or at least to feel guilty if you fail to.

⌒ *I should* go back to school.

⌒ *I should* find out more about that company.

⌒ *I should* check two more stores before I give up.

⌒ Maybe *I should* get a dog.

Even our most mundane language creates. When you claim obligation, you create a picture of yourself in which you are not in charge of your life. Acting on your own desires, you might choose to do the very same things you now do because you *should*. But how might those same actions create different experiences for you if you were acting on your own desires instead of the assumed obligation of *should*?

Consider the familiar ⌒

⌒ I really *should* lose 20 lbs.

Many of us approach fitness issues with a sense of obligation. Whether we are up five pounds or dangerously overweight, we approach the issue—and *state* the issue—the same way. We make our fitness goal a *should* statement rather than stating it as a desire, because we trust obligation to bind us to our goal.

But *should*-diets don't work. Our cheaply fabricated sense of obligation toward what we *should* do often fades quickly. Perhaps we know that whatever we take on because we *should* is not worthy of our full and enduring commitment. Still, we say ⌒

⌒ I *shouldn't* eat that.

I shouldn't does not mean, "I won't." With it, we let Other assert our obligation to do what's "right" and stick to our diet. We invest no self-determination in *I shouldn't*, so it really means, "*I shouldn't*, but I probably will."

Hiding

Each time you claim obligation with *should, have to, must,* or *ought to,* you hide. You deny personal responsibly and in effect, go absent.

⌒ I *have to* pick up my daughter from school.

⌒ I *have to* write my thank-you cards tonight.

⌒ I *have to* meet with my boss to discuss the policy changes.

If you have committed to these things, you could reasonably claim that you are obligated to do them. But your claim of obligation implies that you would not do these things if you were not forced to do them. Implying that you are under duress creates for you an unnecessary experience of obligation.

Let's examine ⌢

⌢ *I have to* pick up my daughter from school.

My daughter is four years old. In some sense it is accurate to say that I am obligated to pick her up. But when I get there she sees me at the door, explodes into a smile, shouts, "Mama!" and runs to me. It's not obligation that brings me to my daughter.

We claim the obligation of *I have to*—nearly always out of unconscious habit—dozens of times each day.

⌢ *I have to* brush my teeth.

⌢ *I have to* go to work.

⌢ *I have to* stop at the store.

⌢ *I have to* make dinner.

Fulfilling an obligation is often no more than the means to an end. We just want to get the job done, often so we can move on to the next obligation. But we short-change ourselves when we act from obligation. Whatever pleasure we might find in these activities is eroded by our sense of obligation to them.

Consider even ⌢

⌢ *I have to* go to the bathroom.

This is the ultimate test of obligation. If you wanted to claim that you were oppressively obligated to go to the bathroom at times—that you *have* absolutely *no choice* in the matter—that you would suffer significant physical unpleasantness if you didn't comply with your natural obligation to empty your body, you could easily support that claim. But you would also experience all of the self-made oppression of that sort of thinking. Just go already.

In this situation we choose to be oppressed by our own bodies. Most of us feed this oppression every day.

The Unseen Oppressor

Each time you rely on the voice of Other with *I should, I have to, I must* or *I ought to,* you choose language that severs you from responsibility.

For example, in ending a phone conversation you may say ⌒

⌒ *I have to* go now.

"*I have to* go," takes the responsibility for ending the conversation away from you and gives it to an Unseen Oppressor—the Other who presumably forces you to hang up the phone. We say we "*have to go,*" so as not to offend the person with whom we are speaking. We fear that saying we "*want* to go" implies that we are eager to be rid of the other person. We choose not to take responsibility for the action, because in this instance, responsibility feels like blame.

Curiously, we often choose to sever ourselves from responsibility even when it means severing ourselves from credit.

Consider a scenario in which you receive an invitation for a night out when you have work to do at home in preparation for a trip the following day.

You might say ⌒

⌒ *I really shouldn't* go out tonight.

Here you manage to escape blame and forfeit credit in one six-word sentence. You avoid the unpleasantness of telling your friend that you intend to choose your work at home over spending time with him, but you also forfeit the opportunity to take credit for making what you hold to be the better choice to complete your work at home. It would be perfectly acceptable for you to assert yourself in this instance—to simply explain that you'd rather not go—but it is always easier to summon the Unseen Oppressor.

Wielding Obligation

When you tell other people what they *should* do, you become the voice of Other. With your guidance, you burden people with a voice other than their own.

We use *you should* to get compliance. But when we want people to do as we ask, we don't usually give much thought to the quality of their compliance. In practice, compliance ranges anywhere from cheerful cooperation to begrudging obedience. But somewhere above even the most satisfying compliance is heart-felt agreement. If our assertion of *you should* draws our listener away from his own voice and onto the voice of Other, he doesn't retain enough of *himself* to muster heart-felt agreement with anything.

Consider ◠

◠ *You should* get a better job.

Here we ask someone to comply with *our* wish. We might even have distracted her from her own desire to change jobs. If we lead with *you should*, any compliance we meet with is tainted by our oppressive interference.

You Must

We sometimes use *you must* to make assumptions about other people, as in ◠

◠ *You must* be so happy!

Though we are not ordering someone to be happy here, we are making the assumption that she *is* happy. But notice what else is at work; we are assuming and inadvertently dictating what we believe to be an acceptable emotional response. We imply that *we* would be happy in her position; therefore, if she is *not* happy, she fails to live up to our standard.

You Ought To

Perhaps the most familiar use of *you ought to* is ⌐

⌐ *You ought to* be ashamed of yourself.

Few of us would think to shame anyone so overtly. But *you ought to* shames, no matter how we use it.

Consider the accusation in ⌐

⌐ *You ought to* be thankful for what you have.

Sometimes we use *you ought to* in slightly less shaming ways, as in ⌐

⌐ *You ought to* see what your mother has to say about that first.

⌐ *You ought to* check the Blue Book price before you buy that car.

⌐ *You ought to* look over those figures one more time.

Here we offer our seemingly innocent advice. But *you ought to* has the feeling of a warning, as if failure to do what we *ought* will earn an "I told you so."

Oppressive Inspiration

One of our most misguided uses of *you have to* occurs when we share our wisdom. If we wish to inspire others with our insights, we may become passionate about the importance of our message. And whether or not we see our way as the *only* way, we may share our insights using language that implies the absolute correctness of those insights. We turn our inspirations into ultimatums when we obligate others to live by our wisdom.

⌐ *You have to* set goals for yourself.

⌐ *You have to* clarify your values.

⌐ *You have to* start planning now for a financially secure retirement.

The people who say these things believe in them passionately, and out of concern for others they become equally passionate about sharing them. This may be an admirable aim, but it is contradicted by the form it takes.

The speaker implies that the things we *have to* do are some sort of minimum requirement for social, personal, and professional competency. If we fail in our obligation to any of these admonitions, what does that say about us?

Oppressive inspiration leaves us hanging. It's one thing to tell us that we *have to* set goals, but it's another to tell us why. Tell us how we benefit from clarifying our values. Tell us what happens when we start planning for a financially secure retirement. Even if a statement of oppressive inspiration is followed by a full explanation of why it is important to adhere to the advice in it, the demeaning effect of the language of oppression makes it impossible for the listener to hear that explanation clearly. Oppressive inspiration delivers the message that we are inadequate, shutting down our ability to receive.

Obligation Creates Opposition

It may seem that the remedy for feeling obligated is to clearly assert a freedom from obligation. Ironically, it's not. Verbal acknowledgment of obligation—whether it is to claim or *dis*-claim it—feeds the obligation, keeping it alive in our experience.

⌐ *I don't have to* tell you where I was.

⌐ *I don't have to* have a permit.

⌐ *I don't have to* fill out that side of the form.

This is the language of opposition. But your opposition—your resistance, denial, and protestation—does not fix what you resist, deny, or protest. Instead it diverts you from your purpose. You move with much greater efficiency toward what you desire if you keep no verbal attachment to whatever it is you wish to leave behind.

Opposition Consciousness

We oppose what displeases us. We see a situation we don't like, and we decide we'd like to create a new and better situation. But when we create from a position of opposition, we create an "opposite." Our intention is to create a situation which is nothing like the original, but in opposition, we create instead another version of it—we create an *opposite-same* of the original situation. In an opposite-same, we create an *opposite* situation through which we experience the *same* unpleasant emotional outcome as in the original.

For example, a child feels dependent upon her family for emotional support, but in the end they fail to support her. As an adult, she wants to create a situation in which she will never again be hurt by a lack of family support. She grows up to form a family of her own, and in her oppositional independence, she limits what she shares with her new family about her ambitions, undermining their ability to support her in them. She intends for her lack of dependence on family support to alleviate the pain of feeling unsupported. But she creates an *opposite* of her childhood situation in which she experiences the *same* lack of support she suffered in childhood.

Another child grows up in a family where his parents' secrets and lies make him feel alone and shut out from the truth. As an adolescent he takes the opposite role—his parents' role—and seeks to make his friends and siblings dependent upon *him*, always eventually shutting them out with his own lies. In his opposite-same, he surrounds himself with people and he is always privy to the truth, but his own lies create for him the same experience of alienation he endured as a child.

A third child feels ugly. As an adult she has multiple plastic surgeries to "improve" her face and body in order to feel beautiful. She recreates herself as an opposite, but she changes her situation without addressing her underlying emotional issues. When she felt ugly, she feared that people were staring at her ugliness. Once she recreates herself as "beautiful" she fears that people are still staring at her, this time wondering how many surgeries she has had. She becomes an *opposite* version of herself, only to continue experiencing the *same* unease she experienced as a child.

In the creation of an opposite-same we may enact an opposite version of some detail of our original situation, we may adopt the behaviors of those we oppose, or we may recreate ourselves as opposites in hopes of experiencing a reversal of our unsatisfying emotional experiences. But Opposition Consciousness always fails us because it is backward-looking. It funnels our energies into opposing problems instead of creating satisfying solutions.

Our oppositional language—*I* don't *have to*—I'll never be like her—I would never marry someone like him—signals that we have an opposite-same in effect. As we create our opposite-sames we feel we're taking responsibility for fixing our own lives. And we are. It's just that we're going about it in a way that fixes nothing. And worse, our new "solutions" keep us content in the notion that our problems are solved while in reality we've postponed a *satisfying* solution indefinitely.

Opposition Consciousness is born in childhood, explodes in adolescence, and often lasts a lifetime. In our oppositions, our overcorrections, our opposite-sames, we become critical of those who criticize others. We become intolerant of intolerance, we feel indignant toward other people's indignation and righteous anger over anyone else's self-righteousness. In these obvious parallels, we can see the illogic of our creations. But in practice, our oppositions feel completely logical and fully justified. When we believe others are wrong we think it's *right* to correct them. When others are unreasonable we think it's our duty to reason with them. But what happens when we do? We rarely change people's opinions by pointing out how wrong or unreasonable they are.

When we accept critical, intolerant, indignant, self-righteous people just as they are, we stop fueling them. When we oppose critical, intolerant, indignant, self-righteous people, we become them. We recreate ourselves as opposite-sames; and we solve nothing.

Acceptance pulls us out of the futile spin of Opposition Consciousness. Once we accept other people just as they are, we cultivate the detachment necessary to see the results of our own oppositions. Then, instead of resisting, denying, protesting, and opposing what we find unsatisfying in our lives, we can fix it.

Self-Portrait: Phase One

Your layers of obligation are muddying your self-portrait. Every time you follow the advice of a *should*-sayer, hide behind the Unseen Oppressor, or oppose what you find distasteful, you add another messy layer of obligation. The more layers you take on, the farther you are from experiencing your true Self.

CHAPTER THREE:
Creating Frustration: Try & Need

Let's explore the limits of *trying*. We'll plot the possibilities of *trying* on a continuum of effort.

On the low end, we have the half-hearted *try*—an attempt so feeble it's likely to escape our notice. (Picture someone reaching for a remote control a few feet away only to stop at the half-way point and give up.) Somewhere in the middle of our continuum we'll find things like *trying* hard, and *trying* our best. On the high end we have "*trying* really really hard" and "*trying* with all our might." (Picture a woman in the final stage of labor. It's time to push, and she's *trying* with all her might to push out that baby. We'll get back to her in a moment.)

With all of our lip service to effort, you'd think there was a big pay-off for *trying*, but there isn't. When we say we'll *try*, we commit to an exertion of effort. That's all.

Now back to our mother-to-be. She's been in labor for half a day and now she's *trying* really really hard to push. I wonder how she'd take the news that *trying* will get her nowhere. It's *pushing*, not *trying* to push, that gets the baby out.

Trying creates frustration by increasing your commitment to effort with no promise to succeed. The more energy you put into your efforts, the less you have left over to put into your accomplishments.

Need creates frustration in a similar way. Let's explore the limits of *need*, also with the help of a continuum.

On the low end of *need*, we find a peaceful lack—the kind we experience when we're out of jelly. No matter how much we like it, we never

31

really *need* it. Much further along, we find less peaceful lacks—perhaps the kind we experience when our car won't start. At the high end of the continuum we'll find desperate lacks—when we're out of oxygen, for example.

No matter what you lack, putting energy into the idea that you *need* it does nothing to move you closer to it. When you claim to be in *need*, you create frustration. The greater your feeling of *need*, the greater your frustration that your *needs* are not being met; and the greater your disadvantage when you eventually pursue what you lack.

Here's an exercise:

1. First think of three things that you absolutely positively *need*.

2. Now consider; are the things you *need*, things you also desire?

You can say accurately that you *need* oxygen, water, and food, but since oxygen, water, and food are essential to your survival, clearly you also desire them. You don't deny that something is essential by calling it a desire; instead, you acknowledge that you desire it rather than lamenting that you *need* it.

Inviting Struggle

I Try

In discussions on the language of oppression, I meet a fair amount of resistance to the elimination of the word *try*. It's the key word in most people's escape clause. *Trying* to lose weight is easier than actually doing it. *Trying* to get a project done on time is a breeze compared to meeting a deadline.

But people also want to keep using *try* because they place an inexplicably high value on effort; they feel that to *try* is noble. While it is true that effort often contributes to accomplishment, many of us lose sight of how much energy we desire to put into each. Remember, *trying* to push doesn't get the baby out; *pushing* does. When you say you are *trying*, you create the experience of striving and struggling, rather than doing what you intend.

A commitment to *try* is also dishonest. It is a smoke screen, under cover of which we can claim faint allegiance to a host of tasks we may or may not have any intention to complete. Despite our most earnest efforts to make it so, *try* almost never means what we intend it to mean. Look at these ‿

‿ *I'm trying* to find a new job.

Translation: Don't look at my progress; just notice my effort.

‿ *I'll try* to be on time tomorrow.

Translation: I commit to worrying about being late.

‿ *I tried.*

Translation: I failed.

It is important to note here that *try* has two meanings, only one of which creates frustration. To *try* means "to strive,"—but it also means "to test."

If you say ‿

‿ *I'm* going to *try* on these shoes—

You mean only that you will *test* the shoes to see if you like their fit, feel, and appearance.

Notice, however, that sometimes both meanings of *try* are in effect at the same time, as in ‿

‿ *I'm* going to *try* this another way.

While you are essentially testing methods in this sentence, some striving is implied. And if you summon struggle to any degree, you create struggle.

You Try

When we ask other people to *try* we do not present them with a peaceful or inspiring challenge. We present them with a request for effort rather than results. We might make a request like ‿

⌐ I just want some indication that you are at least *trying*.

The real message here is "I want to see that you're struggling." Our requests for effort assume a weakness in other people that may have a greater effect on them than we realize. In our petition for effort, we make no mention of what it is we'd like this person to accomplish. And we encourage him to see himself as weak by addressing only his apparent inadequacy.

When the *trying* is over, we often point to effort again, as in ⌐

⌐ Well, at least *you tried*.

Translation: You gave it your best shot, but you failed.

Three Stories About Struggle

1 Horatio Alger wrote popular fiction from the 1850's through the early 1900's. His stories were typically about boys and young men who came from poverty and through hard work, determination, and a fair amount of pulling themselves up by their bootstraps, became productive members of society. These stories were intended to inspire generations of boys to rise above their humble beginnings and to make successes of themselves. But their message was not that if someone was extremely clever, he might achieve success without struggle. The value was primarily on effort, initiative, and struggle, and only secondarily on accomplishment. These stories have determined the ideal American work ethic for well over a century.

2 I once had a boss who announced his retirement. When I expressed interest in taking over his position, he asked me if I was willing to work as hard as he had. Because the question came from someone I respected, I said, "Yes." But later I thought better of it. I supposed I was willing to work as hard as he had, but I questioned whether it was necessary to work as hard as he had worked to accomplish what he had accomplished. He seemed to believe that effort was inherently valuable, and as a result he exhausted himself doing nearly everything he did. I believe that effectiveness is valuable,

and that herculean effort, in situations where efficient action and strategic delegation would yield the same result, is not.

3 A few months into writing this book I quit my job. At first, if someone congratulated me on my decision, I felt compelled to say that even though I no longer had a traditional job, I'd now be *working harder than ever*. (I said it only once. If it had really been my desire to work harder than ever, I'd have gotten a job in a coal mine.) The reality was that writing was (and is) a pleasure, and that it didn't feel like *working harder than ever*. I just wasn't comfortable letting everyone know that.

Many of us are reluctant to let others see our good fortune. We fear being seen as boastful if we tell others that we love our job or our mate or our life. We seem to desire that others see our life as balanced—the good with the bad.

One of the conversations I had shortly after I left my job to write was with an acquaintance I met in the grocery store.

When I told her about my decision she said ∽

∽ It's going to be really hard...

I said sheepishly ∽

∽ It hasn't been hard so far.

She countered ∽

∽ Well, there will be days when you question whether you've made the right decision.

I understood. It's a game we play with ourselves and others; we can only allow success in one area if we give up something somewhere else—or if we struggle.

I am almost certain that if I had said ∽

∽ I feel good about my decision, but it's going to be really hard.

She would have said ∽

∽ If you enjoy what you're doing, it won't even feel like work.

Living With *Need*

Do you sometimes go without the things you *need*? Or are your *needs* always met? Do you consistently have everything you *need*? How would you like to spend three days a week for the rest of your life *trying* to get your *needs* met?

Do you have desires? Are there things you'd like to have? Is there something you'd really like to do? Do you tend to get the things you want? How would you like to spend three days a week for the rest of your life indulging your desires?

You can choose to see anything you lack as either a *need* or a desire. If you claim *need* each time you notice a lack, you will experience deprivation. Most of us do.

I Need

We create *need* before we create effectiveness when we say ‿

‿ *I need* to figure out how to do this.

‿ *I need* a job.

‿ *I need* to find a new dentist.

‿ *I need* some art supplies.

The solution to a lack of art supplies is to get more art supplies— not to lament that you are without them. In each of these examples, *I need* tells you about your deprivation. These examples direct your focus to your problem, which does nothing to move you toward a solution.

We contemplate our own deprivation with the question ‿

‿ What do *I* really *need*?

This has different meanings in different contexts. Whether we are shopping for some trifle or choosing a new home or career or mate, we often ask ourselves what we *need* rather than asking ourselves what we desire. If you operate from a position of *need*, you will usually get your *needs* met. But how satisfying is it to have a *need* met, when that *need* does not reflect what you desire?

36

Beneath our habit of stating our desires as *needs* is the belief that it is wrong to pursue the fulfillment of our desires. If we state our desires *as* desires and pursue their satisfaction, we risk criticism for our self-ishness. It's not our *own* voice that warns us against indulging our desires.

You Need

When we tell others what they *need*, we frustrate them by offering our assessment of what they lack, as in ⌣

⌣ *You need* to take another look at this situation.

⌣ *You need* to get your life in order.

⌣ *You need* a shower.

We offer observations like these in order to be helpful. But here, in the name of helpfulness, we tell someone he's blind to his own situation, his life is a mess, and his hygiene isn't up to snuff.

Even when we mean to lovingly tell others what they *need*, we undermine our message with frustrating language, as in ⌣

⌣ *You need* to know that I care about you.

Here the receiver hears an obligation to change what she knows, before she hears that she is cared for.

You Need My Help

The *you need* statement is often a poorly worded offer of help. In practice, much of what follows *you need* can be harsh. But even when it is followed by a loving suggestion, *you need* is insulting. If it is our habit to concern ourselves with the affairs of our peers, we may increase the deficiencies we perceive in them by "helping" them too much.

In any peer relationship—those of lovers, friends, or acquaintances—we are presumably on equal footing. One does not have the authority to direct; the other does not have an obligation to take direction. But peers sometimes give up their equal footing. And when peers take their seats, one often sits in the helper seat, leaving for the other the seat of *need*. This usually happens without our awareness, and this seating arrangement can remain the same for decades.

You may instinctively take on one of the Helper archetypes: Parent, Teacher, or Therapist. If you play one or more of these roles with any of your would-be peers, you take the helper seat in that relationship. But peer relationships do not flower in this shady arrangement. Even if you are an accomplished guide, the greatest gift you may have for others is the termination of your perpetual help.

An offer of service is, among other things, an accusation that the one we offer to serve is in *need* of that service. We increase the experience of inadequacy in others when we go too far in filling the *needs* we perceive them to have. Our well-intentioned help can magnify someone else's problem, magnifying his sense of inadequacy right along with it.

Look closely at your desires regarding service. Do any of these sound like you?

⌒ I *can't* stand to see others struggle.

⌒ I can handle tough situations better than other people can.

⌒ I am able to help, so I *have to*.

⌒ I like to hear that I am a wonderful helper.

We would like to believe that every time we help someone else, our help is inherently valuable. But the truth is that we don't have good measures of how helpful we are. If we receive gratitude for our efforts, we see that gratitude as a measure of our effectiveness. It isn't. The people we help are grateful for our time and attention; they rarely assesses the quality of our help before offering appreciation.

When we offer our answers, we rob people of devising their own solutions. If their solutions come from us, they won't invest those solutions with the conviction that might otherwise be available to them if they had come up with their solutions on their own.

If you do not want to burden others with your answers, but it is not your desire to turn away those who come looking for your assistance, offer them your support. While ultimately other people will access their own internal answers, you may find yourself in a position to encourage others to look within themselves for the answers they seek. You may help someone to clarify his own values or desires. But question the value of even your most limited guidance. If you find yourself fostering dependence—Do others ask *you* before they ask themselves?—reassess the value of your support.

Trust that others will benefit if you learn to let them sort out their own issues. Trust that other people can handle tough situations. Trust that just because you're able to help, it doesn't mean you *have to*. Realize that you can live without hearing that you are a wonderful helper. And trust that people will still love you even if you stop taking on their problems.

Self-Portrait: Phase Two

Your self-portrait is taking on layers of frustration. Every time you promise to *try*, you invite struggle and you lie about your intentions. When you hide yourself in *need*, you bury your desires. Your portrait looks more anxious with every layer of frustration you put on. The real you beneath the layers is difficult to see.

CHAPTER FOUR

Creating Restriction: Can't & Have No Choice

Here's another exercise:

Finish the sentences below in any way you choose.

1. *I can't*

2. *I can't*

3. *I can't*

⌒ Would you enjoy doing this exercise each morning?

We restrict others by imposing limits on them; we restrict ourselves the same way.

We *can't* keep an appointment—we *can't* reach the top shelf—we *can't* find the pencil we were just using. We tend to use the restrictive word *can't* quite casually. And in doing so, we create the experience of restriction in our lives, perhaps dozens of times each day, without even realizing it.

I have no choice may not be as straight forward as *I can't*. Sometimes we really do *have no choice*. Consider our DNA, for example. There's no changing it. It determines the color of our eyes, hair, and skin. And while we can, of course, change our eye color with contact lenses, dye our hair, and procure any one of several procedures to lighten or darken our skin, our DNA itself is unalterable.

And there are more things in which we *have no choice. I*, for example, *have no choice* in my gender. (Hmm, yes I do, come to think of it.) *I have no choice* in the foreign policy decisions of my country. (Well, not at the moment, but come November I do.) *I have no choice* but to be

Rebecca Smith. (Except that I can change my name and even, to some extent, my identity.) But *I do not have the choice* to be Madonna, because her DNA is already taken. (Though I could probably change my name to Madonna if I really wanted to.)

If you go looking for situations in which you legitimately *have no choice*, you may find a few—but only a few. In reality, you always have a choice, even if you have only *one* choice worth considering. I may not be willing to change my eye color, hair color, skin color, name, or gender, but I can if I choose to. *I have no choice* is nearly always a lie. And that matters.

Self-Talk

Most self-talk that includes *I can't* is the domain of the Unseen Oppressor—the phantom Other who keeps us from doing as we choose. In the first few examples in this section, look for the Unseen Oppressor making the decisions. In later examples, speakers restrict themselves with dependence and opposition.

I Can't

⌐ *I can't* get to the gym after work.

In truth, we say we *can't* when we choose not to. While it may feel true that other obligations keep us from getting to the gym, we could get there if we chose going to the gym over the other activities vying for our time. Here we pretend that someone else forbids us to do as we choose. Our claim of powerlessness denies our self-determination.

I can't also gets us out of our would-be obligations, as in ⌐

⌐ *I can't* make it to your wedding shower.

Again we imply that someone else is keeping us from the event, though we have in fact chosen to do something else. We do not want to disappoint the bride-to-be, so we call upon the Unseen Oppressor to say "no" for us. Instead of taking responsibility, we let the Unseen Oppressor do our dirty work.

We use *I can't* to make dramatic pronouncements of our own weakness, as in ⌣

⌣ *I can't* live without my coffee in the morning!

While this may feel true, it is not. Stating a desire for *anything* as an addiction, magnifies our experience of dependence. We might even intend this statement as a celebration of the life-enhancing qualities of coffee, but we state it as if we are addicts celebrating the "life-enhancing" qualities of heroin.

When *can't* is used as part of a double-negative, it suggests opposition.

Consider ⌣

⌣ I do*n't* see why we *can't* meet you there later.

This is meant as a positive statement, but it is a positive that overcomes a negative. It implies a breaking free from restriction. But breaking free from restriction is nowhere near as satisfying as avoiding it completely.

As we "break free" from something we are likely to take only a momentary glance at it. After our momentary glance leads us to determine that we don't like our situation, we slip into Opposition Consciousness. In opposition to what we don't like, we create an opposite-same—playing out an opposite version of our original situation, adopting the behaviors of those we oppose, or recreating *ourselves* as opposites in hopes of experiencing a reversal of our unsatisfying emotional experiences. Unfortunately, it doesn't work.

Oppositional language, even when used very casually, creates opposition. When you hear yourself use it, realize that you have an opposite-same in effect—or that you are in the act of creating one.

I Have No Choice

The Unseen Oppressor does the dirty work in this section too. Notice again as speaker after speaker denies responsibility for her own actions and lets the Unseen Oppressor act in her "absence."

A police officer answers your plea for leniency with ⌣

⌒ *I have no choice* but to give you a ticket.

A human resources manager says ⌒

⌒ *I have no choice* but to ask for your resignation.

Each speaker puts responsibility for her action onto an Unseen Oppressor. Neither is willing to assert herself, so they both pretend that someone else is responsible for their actions.

We use *I have no choice* with our children when we do not want to experience our full responsibility as parents.

Consider ⌒

⌒ *I have no choice* but to punish you for skipping school.

Ideally we administer discipline to our child because we think it helps him remember not to repeat his mistake. To claim in this situation that we *have no choice* is to absent ourselves from a very important moment. Our love for our children takes a back seat to the oppression of *I have no choice*. When we go absent in these situations, we miss the opportunity to be fully available to our children.

Restricting Others

You Can't

With *you can't*, we tell people either that we won't let them do as they wish or that they are not equal to accomplishing what they wish to do.

⌒ *You can't* do that.

⌒ *You can't* keep making the same mistakes again and again.

⌒ *You can't* expect to make it as a rock star.

You can't is a hammer of oppression. It's hurtful, argumentative, and avoidable.

You Have No Choice

You have no choice denies another person's right to act, and we use it to get compliance. With it we may get the compliance we seek, but not without some cost to our integrity. When we deny others their options, we ask them to put their own desires aside, leaving no possibility for heart-felt agreement. We belittle the person whose choices we limit. If we do get the compliance we are after, we get the compliance of a broken person.

Often we restrict others because we feel restricted. When we experience restriction and do not reconcile our emotions around that experience, we may thoughtlessly repeat that pattern of restriction on others. We follow the opposite-same model of father-kicks-son—son-kicks-dog. When we create from our habits, we ride the momentum of those habits without considering the consequences.

Consider ⌐

⌐ You're going to camp this summer, Billy; *you have no choice!*

How happy do you suppose Billy is going to be at summer camp?

Self-Portrait: Phase Three

Layers of restriction are the heaviest of all. If your paints haven't muddied before now, they will in this phase. It's impossible to experience restriction and not be marked by it. Thick layers of restriction suffocate everything beneath them.

Are you ready to grab a scraper?

PART THREE

Solutions

"Do not seek yourself outside yourself."
—Ralph Waldo Emerson

CHAPTER FIVE
Transcending Obligation: Should, Have to, Must & Ought to

Our use of the language of obligation guarantees the experience of obligation in our lives. Through our thoughtless repetition of it, this language hypnotizes us into believing in its accuracy. When we eliminate the language of obligation, the power of its trance ends, and we transcend obligation.

When obligation disappears, it makes room for desire. Every time you hear yourself say, *"I should,"* stop and ask yourself, "What do I desire?"

When I began making changes in my own language, trading obligation for desire felt revolutionary. And while it made me feel self-indulgent, I felt entitled to that indulgence. That's when I noticed that my new definition of desire, one no longer loaded with emotional connotations, had become practical. I wasn't asking myself about some theoretical notion of desire—I wasn't asking about the desires of others—I was asking about my own desires. And in the day-to-day, my own desires were pretty tame.

In fact, when I began trading obligation for desire, I noticed that I rarely changed my actions. If I used to go to the post office because I *had to*, I'd now go to the post office because I wanted to. If I heard myself saying, *"I have to run to the store,"* I stopped and asked myself what I really wanted to do. If running to the store wasn't at the top of my list, I'd measure one desire against another. "I'd like to stay home and read," I might reason, "But I'm out of juice, and I'd like some for my breakfast." I'd look for a *desire* to run to the store, and if I found one, I'd go.

Those small moments of *self-reference*—the half-dozen times each day that I referred to myself and did what I desired—accumulated. Each time I chose to indulge a desire rather than to act on an obligation, I felt a little more free. And until I began to leave my slavish devotion to obligation behind, I never realized how thoroughly it had shaped my life.

As you begin to replace obligation with desire you will have moments of groping for words that better reflect your situation. You can experience those moments as awkward verbal stumbling, or you can see them as the priceless moments you spend looking for ways to express yourself more authentically.

Perhaps it would be enough to simply reword statements of obligation as statements of non-obligation. Certainly you would improve the shape of your life if every time you were tempted to say *I should*, you said instead *I could, I might, I will*, or *I want to*. But restatement is not always enough. There is a disingenuousness in the *should* stance that takes more than the rewording of your thoughts to eliminate.

I should, I have to, I must, and *I ought to* are the voice of Other. As you eliminate the voice of Other, you will begin to hear the voice of Self.

Fixing Our Self-Talk

Eliminating *I Should*

- *I should* go back to school.

- *I should* find out more about that company.

- *I should* check two more stores before I give up.

- Maybe *I should* get a dog.

This is the voice of Other; it is not your own voice. The next time you hear yourself say, "*I should,*" pause. Ask yourself, "What do I *desire?*"

As you take on the elimination of the language of obligation, choose to see every *should* as an opportunity to refer to yourself. Each time you hear yourself claiming obligation, ask yourself what you want most in that moment. At first you will ask yourself about small things; after a while, you will encounter your deeper desires. Over time, you will trade the stance of one mired in obligation for the stance of one who acts responsibly on his or her own desires.

Look again at one of our statements of obligation.

⌒ I *should* go back to school.

If you proceed from the question, "What do I desire for my decision about school?" some of your choices for rewording this statement are as follows ⌒

⌒ I'm thinking about going back to school.

⌒ I want to go back to school.

⌒ I'm going back to school.

Each of these re-statements removes the sense of obligation. Each, however, accomplishes something different. While your immediate objective is to remove obligation from what you say, your ultimate objective is to reshape each of your ideas in a way that allows you to acknowledge yourself as the source of those ideas.

Consider the options ⌒

⌒ I'm thinking about going back to school.

Here you begin to claim responsibility with a return to yourself. You no longer act on the assumed wishes of an internalized voice that says you *should*. You do, however, lack a strong sense of self-determination with "I'm thinking about." Depending upon the delivery, this may sound like you are floating an idea to see how it's received.

So how about ⌒

⌒ I want to go back to school.

This option has more self-determination. Here you state what *you* want to do, not what you believe someone else thinks you *should* do. This is an improvement as it leaves behind the *should* stance and reveals your own desires.

The word *want*, however, has at least two meanings, and they create very different effects. To want something can mean to desire it, but to want something can also mean to *lack* it. When you question yourself with, "What do I really want?" you inquire predominantly about your desire. When you say, "I want somebody to take care of me," you more clearly affirm lack. If you remain conscious of these distinctions, you can use *want* to create only the effects you desire.

In the case of, "I want to go back to school," determine for yourself what the effect is. If the energy behind a statement beginning with *I want* is timid, the speaker reveals her doubt and conveys weakness. If it sounds like a strong statement of intention, the speaker and listener will both experience *I want* as *I desire*.

Now consider our last revision ⌣

⌣ I'm going back to school.

With personal responsibility and self-determination, with no test-ing of the waters, no self-doubt or room for questioning, you state your intention to do as you desire.

I am is the most potent expression of Self in the English language. When you follow it with an expression of your intention, it scrapes away a layer or two of your identification with obligation, invariably creating a more authentic experience of *yourself*. When you say *I am*, you fortify your position with a strong affirmation of presence.

It is important to remember also that your self-referential ques-tioning may lead you to do something counter to what you once thought you *should* do. If upon careful consideration of your wishes you decide you do not want to resume school, it is perfectly accurate to say ⌣

⌣ I am not going back to school.

The other examples at the beginning of this section can be reshaped using the same model of eliminating obligation to Other and stating a more personal desire in its place.

⌣ *I should* find out more about that company.

Ask yourself instead, "Do I want to find out more about the company?" If your answer is "yes" then pursue it, with ⌒

⌒ I will find out more about that company.

I will, like *I am*, is a potent affirmation of presence. It creates self-determination as it promises action.

⌒ *I should* check two more stores before I give up.

Says who? Do you want to spend the time? Is it worth it to you? Figure out what you want to do, and then voice it.

⌒ I'm going home. Maybe I'll call the other two stores when I'm not so tired.

It's only shopping. If you are going to do the task anyway, pull the obligation out of it. If this task was legitimately invested with challenges and deadlines, you could still say ⌒

⌒ *I'm going to* check two more stores.

Consider finally ⌒

⌒ Maybe *I should* get a dog.

Do you desire to have a dog? It's not a right-or-wrong decision. If you weigh your pros and cons and decide you want a dog, indulge your desire to have one.

Self-Indulgence

If we heard without context the statement, "That guy is really self-indulgent," most of us would wonder what sort of decadence he had been indulging in. While there is nothing in the definition of self-indulgent to imply that it is inherently negative or harmful, we use the term most often as an insult.

Our leeriness of self-indulgence reveals our fundamental mistrust of the Self. We are, after all, a culture that celebrates self-discipline and self-lessness and looks with suspicion at self-promotion and self-reverence.

We forget that self-indulgence can apply to the indulgence of our most loving desires. With this somewhat specialized definition of self-indulgence in mind, consider the notion that it may be through thoughtful self-indulgence that we express ourselves most authentically.

Our authentic desires can be modest or life-altering. They might look like any of these:

- I'm going to make my living as an artist.
- I know I've always helped, but next time I'm saying, "No."
- I'm quitting my job to do volunteer work full time.
- I want to experience what it's like to be physically fit.

Some of us are indoctrinated with the belief that it is selfish, dangerous, or even sinful to indulge our desires. But look closely at your desires. Are they destructive? Are they harmful to others? If you think you have harmful desires, but you haven't been acting on them, maybe they aren't as strong as you fear.

Most of us use the language of oppression to justify indulging our desires. If we say we *should* or we *have to* indulge, then we can blame the Unseen Oppressor for making us indulge ourselves.

Consider these

- *I need* to sit down for a minute.
- *I have to* buy a new suit for my brother's wedding.
- *I should* get a massage one of these days.

We are more comfortable saying that we *need to, should,* and *have to* do these things than we are admitting that we want to do them. But why? Look again:

- I want to sit down for a minute.
- I'm buying a new suit for my brother's wedding.
- I'd like to get a massage one of these days.

Whose voice tells you that you *shouldn't* sit down until all of your work is done? Whose voice says you *should* be perfectly happy and grateful to wear what you already have in your closet? Whose voice tells you that you *shouldn't* get a massage when you could send that money to the Red Cross?

We fear our self-indulgence because we don't believe we can be trusted to indulge ourselves appropriately. It may sound prudent to be vigilant of our own capacity for excess, but by whose standard are we judging that excess, that prudence, or that appropriateness? It is not our *own* voice that tells us we are not to be trusted.

Look honestly at your indulgences, and decide for yourself whether they accurately reflect your values. It is a matter of individual integrity.

When you consider the pursuit of self-indulgence, you may be tempted to assess *other* people's indulgences. You may look at the person next to you and bristle at the thought of that person indulging his or her desires. But this is about you. When you look into other peoples' lives you are like the student looking for information on his classmate's paper. In life, though, the teacher has fooled us; no two students have been given the same assignment.

Desire

Catching yourself in the act of *should*-saying provides you with an opportunity to tap into your desires. In instances where you might have taken on life-changes out of obligation, you can now commit to them as indulgences of your desires.

Consider ∽

∽ I really *should* lose 20 lbs.

Here you have the opportunity to ask yourself, "What do I desire for the state of my body?" If the answer comes back, "I desire to be fit and healthy," you can joyfully take on the practices that indulge your desire to be fit and healthy.

Trade obligation for determination and say ∽

∽ I am going to lose 20 lbs.

or ∽

∽ I am losing 20 lbs.

The voice of Other says *I should*; your own voice says *I am*.

Our Puritanical roots encourage us to keep a tight reign on our desires. Our desires are suspect, as if following them were likely to get us into trouble. Many spiritual paths would have us transcend desire entirely—to move beyond it into pure and selfless Being. But even if transcending desire is your ultimate goal, you won't transcend desire by opposing it. The path that leads beyond desire runs *through* it, not around it.

Explore desire. Express it in as many ways as you like. *I desire* is not so different from ⌒

- ⌒ I want—
- ⌒ I would like—
- ⌒ I would enjoy—
- ⌒ It would please me to—

With greater attention on your desires, you will more confidently distinguish your passing whims from your desires. Whims, wishes, and flights of fancy pop into your head, and some of them feel a lot like desires. You may even get an *idea* that you mistake for a desire. You may label that idea as "good," and you may follow it for some time before realizing you've been indulging a "good idea" rather than an authentic desire. There is no formula for knowing a desire from a whim, wish, or idea. But the more time you spend asking yourself about your desires, the more adept you will become at recognizing a desire when you feel one.

For now, the blur in which many of our desires reside keeps us from recognizing them. They flitter in and out of our complete or partial consciousness and we may pay very little attention to them. But our desires are useful. The actions we take that have strong, clear desires at their foundation are far more likely to succeed than actions founded on thoughtless whims, vague notions of what's *right*, reluctant compliance, or an automatic deference to the wishes of others.

Eliminating *I Have To*

⌣ *I have to* pick up my daughter from school.

Instead of claiming *I have to* pick up my daughter, I'll say ⌣

⌣ I'm *going to* pick up my daughter from school.

or even ⌣

⌣ I *get to* pick up my daughter from school!

I'll ask myself, "What do I desire in this moment?" With one self-referential question, the act of picking up my daughter is transformed from an obligation into an opportunity to indulge my desire to see my daughter.

We claim obligation in dozens of ordinary tasks every day.

⌣ *I have to* brush my teeth.

⌣ *I have to* make dinner.

⌣ *I have to* go to the bathroom.

Why not, simply ⌣

⌣ I'm going to brush my teeth.

⌣ I'm making dinner.

and ⌣

⌣ I'll be right back.

Some people's thoughts surface as understandable sentences; some people's don't. Even if you don't announce your every move, notice your feelings in such matters—notice your stance. You may feel obligation as you carry out your everyday tasks even when you don't voice it. If you feel that you are going about your daily business mired in obligation, stop yourself. Ask yourself what you desire in each instance. Carry out the same activities as indulgences of your desire.

Eliminating *I Must*

⌐ *I must* get to work on time today.

The question to ask is, "Do I *desire* to get to work on time?" Perhaps you can get to work on time not because you are obligated to do so, but because it *feels* better to be on time than it does to be late.

Eliminating *I Ought To*

⌐ *I ought to* make some plans for my trip.

Do you not also *want* to make plans for your trip? Even if it's a trip you dread, you can still choose not to add obligation to it.

It may seem like denial to state that you *want to* do something that you really do feel obligated to do. With some thought, though, you may conclude that a nagging obligation is more painful than whatever action it takes to cross that obligation off your list. If you play one desire off the other—"Would I rather make my plans or would I rather worry about *not* making my plans?"—you may find that your desire to plan your trip outweighs your desire to put if off. Especially in instances where you've decided that you *are* going to move forward with an action, focus on the fact that you've chosen that action, and avoid claiming obligation in pursuit of it. No matter how much you dread making the plans, it is still accurate to say ⌐

⌐ I'm going to plan my trip.

Sometimes we oppress ourselves with statements of past obligation—or worse yet, statements of a failure to have met past obligations. These are not so easy to restate. Consider ⌐

⌐ *I ought to* know better by now.

We'd benefit from releasing not only this phrase, but all the beliefs behind it. The closest approximation of a restatement I can think of that does not feel like self-blame is ⌐

⌐ Oops.

Ethics

Ethics is the study of what is *right* in a generally agreed-upon sense. The very nature of ethical discussion cultivates both the *im*personal-ization of actions and a sense of obligation to act ethically.

I was struck by this notion as I listened to a radio call-in program which featured the writer of a weekly column on ethics. He spoke again and again of our "ethical obligation" to whatever course of action was up for discussion.

Listening to him led me to consider how ethics influence those who embrace them. Who acts ethically, and why? Who benefits, and in what way?

Let's begin with a definition, straight out of *Webster's New Universal Unabridged Dictionary*.

> **Ethics** (eth′iks), *n.pl.* 1. a system of moral principles; *the ethics of a culture.* 2. the rules of conduct recognized in respect to a particular class of human actions or a particular group, culture, etc.: *medical ethics; Christian ethics.* 3. moral principles, as of an individual; *His ethics forbade betrayal of a confidence.* 4. that branch of philosophy dealing with values relating to human conduct, with respect to the rightness and wrongness of certain actions and to the goodness and badness of the motives and ends of such actions.

Three of the four definitions (all but the 3rd) speak of principles, rules, values, right, wrong, good, and bad as if these principles, rules, values, and judgements were common to all. Largely, they are. We do commonly agree that it is *wrong* to lie, steal, or injure others. (Most of us also agree that there are some extreme circumstances when it would be *right* to lie, steal, or injure others.) The principles, rules, and values we agree upon as a culture have become our collective ethics in part because they help us to live more harmoniously.

So what (if any) is our obligation to the principles, rules, and values of our collective ethics? Do we merely uphold these principles, rules, and values because it's *right* to do so? Do we act ethically because it is our *obligation* to act ethically?

Obligation binds us, and we seek that bond because it makes us feel safe. We feel that if we are obligated to a standard, we will not fail to uphold it. But a bond of obligation distorts the intention behind our actions. Acting because we *have to* precludes our acting because we personally value the action. Our most powerful intentions come from the Self. But our deference to ethical obligation causes us to put on a layer of obligation before we act, distancing us from our own intentions.

I was, throughout my childhood and well into my adult life, a rule-follower. I believed that *I'm-doing-what's-right-because-it's-the-right-thing-to-do* was an admirable stance. But my stance was missing one thing—me. What role did my own values play in the act of *doing-what's-right*? How *personal* an act is it to learn a set of rules or to follow it?

Let's look again at the influence of ethics—this time as it applies to the *doing-what's-right* stance: Who acts ethically, and why? Who benefits, and in what way?

While operating from the *doing-what's-right* stance, I was acting ethically because I thought it made me a good person, because I feared being seen as anything other than a good person, and because I knew that if I acted *un*ethically and something bad happened, I'd have a lot more to answer for than I would if I'd acted ethically.

And who benefited? Nobody. While my deference to ethics made sure I didn't spend my time lying, stealing, or injuring people, it did nothing to move me beyond this minimum level of social competency. And perhaps more importantly, there was anxiety in my *doing-what's-right-because-it's-right*. I believed that others would only love me if I did what was right, and I believed that I would only do what was right if I *had to*.

Back then I saw ethics as a complete guide for living. Now I see ethics as a valuable point of departure. Unfortunately, few people trust themselves enough to depart from ethics into more personal expressions of loving action. Few people trust that their own desire to express love in the world will lead them to act "ethically."

So what is the influence of love on action? Who acts from love, and why?

The individual who consistently listens to his *own* voice acts from love because his emotions are clear enough for him to realize that it *feels* better to take care of the poor than it does to let them suffer, that it *feels* better to de-escalate a situation than it does to fight, and that it *feels* better to buy something than it does to steal it.

And who benefits? All benefit.

In practice, ethics and love will often lead you to the same compassionate action. But as long as you depend on ethics to guide you, you hold your own capacity for loving action at arm's length. Trust yourself to do what's loving because you value loving action.

Talking to Others

We use *you should* to advise people. But in our peer relationships— those in which we are in no way responsible for the behavior of others—we have no business advising anyone.

Consider who benefits from your elimination of *you should*. The person to whom you speak has one fewer person acting as the voice of Other. But *you* benefit even more from discontinuing your use of *you should* on other people. Your use of *you should* sets you up to *be* the voice of Other. That means you're responsible for making sure other people do what you think is *right*. You *have to* be vigilant of other people's actions. You *have to* monitor them to be sure they're doing what they *should*. Being the voice of Other is exhausting. Fortunately, you are not obligated to be the voice of Other.

Talking with Children

Some of our most cherished relationships are with children. The way we ask our children to do things influences how they make requests of others. If we give them mandates without options they learn to do the same with us and others. In most instances you can choose instead to lead a child back to himself. When you provide children with information, you give them the opportunity to agree. More often than not, you can include your child in decision-making. Even when that's not your desire, you can still shape your language to respect the individuality and promote the self-determination of children.

Consider ⌒

⌒ *You have to* take your medicine.

This is essentially bad news, stated oppressively. Remove the oppressive element and add information that might lead the child to agree, as in ⌒

⌒ Here's the medicine that makes your nose stop running.

In this new construction you show respect for the child's ability to partner with you. You remind him why he has medicine to take, and you provide him with an opportunity to choose to cooperate—rather than an obligation to do as you command. In this example his compliance is mandatory, but you leave no room for agreement when you state it as such. Your aim is twofold: you want the child to take his medicine, but you also want him to decide for *himself* to take the medicine. If you desire the ideal, provide a situation in which the ideal is possible.

Trade ⌒

⌒ *You have to* eat your vegetables before you eat dessert.

for ⌒

⌒ It's the vegetables that keep you strong and healthy.

Trade ⌒

⌒ *You have to* be in bed by 8:00.

for ⌒

⌒ Let's get you into bed by 8:00 so you won't be tired tomorrow.

Lose the language of oppression and replace it with information that makes agreement possible.

Our struggles with older children and adolescents are often about the use of their time. Discussions about what we expect from them are more effective when they include clarification of how they (as competent individuals) can manage their time effectively in order to accomplish what we ask them to accomplish. If you want your older children to do as you ask, and further, to decide of their own volition to do as you ask, put into place all of the components for that to happen. This means that you discuss and agree upon not only what you expect children to do, but also how they will *manage themselves* to do it.

Consider this example: You have delegated to an older child the task of taking out the garbage. She has done it a few times, but she doesn't seem to notice when the can is full, and you've found yourself telling her every time she is to take the garbage out. You want her to notice when the can is full and to take out the garbage without being asked.

You could initiate a discussion this way ⌐

⌐ Whenever I ask you to take the garbage out, you do it. I appreciate that.

⌐ (look of surprise)

⌐ Can we put into place a system where you take the garbage out without being asked?

⌐ What do you mean? Why would I do that?

⌐ I'd just like to add to the job of taking out the garbage, that you also notice when the can is full and empty it without being asked.

⌐ (look of bafflement)

⌐ Could you look at the can every day and decide when it's full and take it out if it is?

⌐ How can I tell if it's full or not?

⌐ I think you can tell. *Do you realize that you won't be taking it out any more than you do now? The only difference will be that I won't be asking you to do it every time.*

Whatever happens next, you've asked for what you want and you've given enough information for the child to decide on her own to do as you ask. You've offered *her* the opportunity to be the voice that says, "It's time to take out the garbage," and you've indicated that if it comes from her, it won't come from you.

Children of any age do not often see themselves as partners in negotiation and as a result they comply (at best) but rarely have presence enough to agree with your requests. You can help nurture a child's voice by modeling your own self-referential questioning and by offering the child the opportunity for heartfelt agreement with every request you make.

Gracefully Receiving Statements of Obligation

Once you decide to take charge of your habits of language, you will begin to notice when others imply that you are still oppressed by obligation. While these instances are common enough to have previously escaped your notice, they will escape it no longer.

It is important to note that you benefit most by concerning yourself with your *own* habits of language. You may always notice the language of oppression when used by others, but there is no reason to let it offend you. Just as it was an unconscious verbal habit for all of us to claim obligation for ourselves and others, it remains an unconscious verbal habit for the vast majority of people.

When others offer you obligation, gently state a desire without correcting the other person.

For example, if a friend at work sees that you are overwhelmed and says ⌒

⌒ *You should* really take a vacation.

You could answer ⌒

⌒ I think I might like that.

While you might previously have answered, "Yes, I probably *should*," your new stance ignores the imposed obligation and moves you forward with a nod to your own desires.

If an opportunity to gracefully assert a desire after someone has claimed obligation for you does not present itself, let it go. Continue to set an example with your own speech.

Obligation Addiction—and Recovery

When I was in high school I *had to* have a job because I *had to* have a car. I *had to* have a car because I *had to* be on time so I wouldn't inconvenience anyone. And I *had to* be able to get to my friends because they *needed* me.

At that time I had heavy expectations on me at home as well. My chores were endless, and I was at the beck and call of my quick and enterprising mother; I *had to* do everything she asked of me, and I *had to* do it immediately.

Near the end of my junior year a friend told me about a man who *needed* a secretary. He hired me. That meant that I had two jobs—as well as school, friends, and my obligations at home. I saw, of course, no possibility of taking time for myself. I didn't even know what that meant.

I worked both jobs and went to school and did all of my housework for the next several months. By July, the summer of my 17th year, I had developed mononucleosis.

In those days mono meant a month in bed—no activities at all. It meant I was restricted from going to work, restricted from visiting friends, restricted from doing any work at home, and restricted from leaving the close confines of my hot, stuffy bedroom.

But it also meant that for an entire month, no one could ask me for anything.

At the time, the irony of my situation was lost on me—a month in solitary confinement promised more freedom than the life I'd been living. It was, up until fairly recently, the best month of my life.

That July, I got a message from my body. Since it had been impossible for me to say "no" to anyone, I *had to* get sick to have an excuse to sit down.

As an adolescent I had no sense of myself as separate from my family. I functioned as a limb of that unit. Elsewhere in the world I shaped my relationships in a way that paralleled what I'd learned in my family. (Until we gain some consciousness about our original learning, we all do this. It's what we do before we figure out how to make ourselves even more miserable with Opposition Consciousness.) I felt excessively obligated in my family, so I made sure I felt as obligated as possible at school and work.

Adolescence presents the opportunity of a lifetime for an obligation addict—I was miserable myself (40 extra pounds, stringy hair, acne) and still got to spend countless hours counseling and comforting my equally miserable friends.

But the physical weakness I cultivated in myself after my bout with mono got me out of things. It was my free pass to set boundaries, which I did by looking run down enough for my mother to send me to bed. I had learned that the only way I'd get to sit down was if I demonstrated that I couldn't stand up. My family accepted my sudden frailty in the same way a person would slow his walking if his knee hurt. I was part of the family body, completely undifferentiated, and the only way I could figure out to be separate was to be sick—the limb that fails in its obligation to the rest of the body.

I did not learn, in that month of mononucleosis, the lesson my body meant to teach me. As a result I had ailments of varying degrees of severity (always in times of stress) for the next twenty years. But I understand the lesson now. Our bodies are living organisms, and like all living organisms, they function for self-preservation. If I don't get the message that stress is ruining my life the first 237 times, my body will continue to attempt delivery until someone is home.

When we see ourselves as parts of a family unit—as its limbs rather than as individuals within that unit—we invariably feel oppressed by that unit. If we come from family situations where we feel oppressed, we find situations outside of our families in which we feel that familiar oppression, and we learn (perhaps most importantly) to lie to ourselves about it. In order to avoid facing the truth, we continue our original patterns, and we continue to see them as normal until we become consciousness of what we learned in our families.

But coming to consciousness means self-examination, and we fear self-examination because we fear the truth about what happened to us.

Further, if what happened to us does not include a holocaust of one sort or another, we feel ourselves at risk for criticism as whiners. But taking a look at what we learned in our families has value no matter what we find. We aren't looking back to see how our parents screwed us up. We're looking back to find clues about why we do what we do.

My lack of differentiation from my family made it impossible for me to see the extent to which I was obligating myself to other people. I was nearly 40 before it occurred to me that just because I *could* help, didn't mean I *had to*. While that information hit me like a lightning bolt, it didn't instantly reshape my life. For some time to follow, I still over-extended myself. It took some time to run the new me (the one who had this liberating information) through all of my current life-situations. How would my new liberation affect my relationships at work? How would it affect my friendships, my relationship with my parents, my siblings, my husband, my child?

Even when the big answers come, nothing changes until *we* change. If the day ever comes when someone taps you on the head and says, "There. Now you're enlightened," you can be sure that the next thing out of her mouth will be, "And you have the rest of your life to figure out what to do about it."

Self-Portrait: Phase Four

Take a deep breath and start scraping. Scrape your layers of obligation away and wipe off your scraper on a newspaper. Throw the paper away.

As soon as you notice yourself taking on layers of obligation, scrape them off. Here's how it works: The thought, "*I have to* get my car washed," pops into your head. At that moment your brush is drenched in paint and you smear a layer of obligation onto your portrait. Then you pause and replace that thought with, "What do I *want to* do about my dirty car?" Your self-referent question puts the scraper in your hand. You answer, "I *like* having a clean car; I *want to* wash my car." Your self-indulgent answer scrapes off the layer of obligation—and a few more layers along with it.

With obligation out of the way, desire returns. We begin to recall who we are when we tap into what we want. Dip your brush into your favorite color and paint a desire on your canvas. Scrape it off and notice how much more beautiful the imprint has already become.

CHAPTER SIX

Transcending Frustration: Try & Need

Frustration is a complex force. It somehow manages to spin us into urgent motion while paralyzing us at the same time.

When frustration feels normal to us, we're stuck in an on-going spin of half-conscious volition. We allow our energies to wander into vaguely desperate contemplations of what we lack and to our senseless commitments to struggle, leaving us less emotional energy and a diminished sense of Self.

While most of us would say that we *avoid* frustration, we tell ourselves stories about our frustrations every day. If we're serious about avoiding frustration, we'll avoid using the language of it.

When we cease to struggle, we experience competence. When we leave behind the notion of *need*, we experience wholeness.

Releasing Struggle

Eliminating *I'll Try*

The *I'll try* stance conveys a lack of confidence. *I'll try*, followed by whatever statement of intention, creates *trying* before it creates anything else. That *trying* takes energy, and it takes its energy from you.

To move beyond the *I'll try* stance, examine what language might better reflect your specific intention. If you'd prefer to put energy into what you intend to accomplish, avoid first depleting that energy with *trying*.

⌐ *I'll try* to be on time tomorrow.

When you state your intention to *try*, you send a mixed message. *Try* throws your listener's focus off of your intention to get to work on time and onto the effort itself. It's as if we're seeking credit for our efforts. But remember what damning praise it is to hear, "Well, at least you *tried*."

The *I'll try* stance is also dishonest as we use it to promise action while it really promises only effort.

If you really do intend to be on time, you'll say ⌒

⌒ I'll be on time tomorrow.

You may occasionally feel reluctant to state categorically that you will do one thing or another. You may fear that you will not live up to your promise to succeed. Admittedly, there are some instances in which a promise to succeed is not reasonable. If someone asks you to promise something that you truly do not know whether you can deliver, you can promise your best and leave it at that.

Recall also that *try* has two possible meanings. The meaning, "to test," creates no frustration; the other *try* promises the frustration of striving. Occasionally both meanings are in effect simultaneously, as in ⌒

⌒ I'm going to *try* this another way.

Though you are essentially testing methods in this sentence, you can remove the implication of striving by avoiding the promise to *try*, as in ⌒

⌒ I'm going to *do* this another way.

The *I'll try* stance spins us like a top. We promise to put ourselves into motion without promising (even to ourselves) that we will get anywhere. Trading the *I'll try* stance for an *I will* stance opens you to forward movement.

Eliminating *You Try*

We place people in an awkward position when we ask them to *try*. We mean for them to do their best, but all we really ask for is a show of effort, as in ⌒

⌐ Please *try* harder next time.

Asking people to make an effort does not help their effectiveness. If you focus on effort over effectiveness, so will they. You could trade ⌐

⌐ Please *try* harder next time.

for something more specific, like ⌐

⌐ This is what I'd like you to accomplish by Friday:—

The *you try* stance is inherently problematic. If what you're after is not effort, but effectiveness, appeal to the other person's competence. Remind him of what he's good at by tailoring your request to his strengths.

If, for example, you've been asking for a show of effort from a child struggling with a new math skill, you might say ⌐

⌐ You're very good at multiplication. I'd like you to focus on that for a little while longer before you move on to fractions.

It is ironic that we ask people to *try* in order to encourage them. Remember the axiom, "If at first you don't succeed, *try, try* again." (If you do the math on that one, you'll see that its unfortunate ratio is three *tries* to one potential success.)

Put some attention on the matter at hand, and ask for what you want. If you really do want to see that someone is making an effort, ask for a show of effort—but realize that you have not asked for the successful completion of anything.

Eliminating *He, She & They Try*

Discussing the efforts of *others* is inherently speculative, generally pointless, and often unkind. When we talk about other people's efforts, we inadvertently point to their failures.

We might believe we are giving a compliment with ⌐

⌐ *He tries* harder than anyone I know.

But we're not. We merely imply that he expends a lot of effort—perhaps more than others would use to get the same amount accomplished. We could make a much clearer statement of our admiration with ⌣

⌣ He dedicates himself fully to everything he does.

Gracefully Receiving Requests for Effort

When someone asks you to *try*, state your intention to succeed.

If someone asks you ⌣

⌣ Will you *try* to make it to my event?

You could answer ⌣

⌣ I'll do my best to be there.

If someone points to your having previously *tried* (and failed), own up to the situation as best you can.

⌣ You *tried* to put together a group to go to Brazil last year, didn't you?

You could answer ⌣

⌣ Yes.

It would be obnoxious to argue the point of whether or not you *tried*. In this instance the other person's use of the word is accurate, if somewhat unflattering.

Inviting Desire

Eliminating *I Need*

The effect of habitually saying *"I need"* is that we feel *needy*. Even if you would not think to apply the term *needy* to yourself, how many times will you say *"I need"* before your subconscious gets the message that you are, in fact, *needy*? When you stop claiming *need*, you make room for desire.

Consider the casual expression ⌒

⌒ *I need* to figure out how to do this.

Needing, like *trying*, takes energy, and it takes its energy from you. Focus your creative energy on effectiveness with ⌒

⌒ I'm going to figure out how to do this.

or better yet ⌒

⌒ I'm figuring out how to do this.

When you move from *"I need"* to *"I am,"* you move your attention from the problem to the solution.

Occasionally even your self-referential questioning may take a frustrating turn, as in ⌒

⌒ What do I really *need*?

You are always free to ask yourself what you desire rather than what you *need*. Still, the question, "What do I really *need*?" is worth looking at.

In reshaping this question, beware of obligation-wielding imitations like ⌒

⌒ Is this what's *best* for me?

You're on a better track here—checking with yourself more gently, shedding the overt frustration of *need*. But the idea of what is "best" for you is not necessarily a reflection of your own desires. Your *should-sayers* have been telling you what's best for you for years. You can take a less frustrating, more personal stance with ⌒

⌒ What would satisfy me?

or a strong and self-reflective ⌒

⌒ What do I want?

Statements of personal *need* tend to be some of our most emotionally loaded expressions of self-oppression. Feel the emotions these *need*-statements evoke; then return to yourself and find words that accurately convey the desires they've been hiding.

I Need You

A statement of our own *need* can reach powerfully into the lives of others. In romantic relationships especially, our focus on *need* creates a perilous imbalance.

To *need* a loved one is to place an obligation on that person. We often claim *need* rather than desire because we feel we have a right for our *needs* to be met, but we feel guiltily self-indulgent when we put our desires out for fulfillment. But a loving relationship is no place for such timidness. In love, as always, our desires are as legitimate as our *needs*.

If we choose to say we *need* our loved one, perhaps we are simply using the dramatic language of film or literature. When the male lead says to his lover, "You complete me," we melt. Unless we are thinking. Ideally, mates are individually whole, and neither depends upon the other for completion.

It is an illusion that mutual *need* assures permanence in relationships. If we infect our romantic relationships with *neediness*, we oppress each other with feelings of obligation. We fear that we will lose our mate if our mate does not feel obligated to us, when it is far more likely that we will drive away a mate on whom we impose obligation.

We claim *need* in relationships because it feels binding. We feel comforted by the presence of something outside of us that we think will cement our connection to one another. But our sense of obligation to our mate comes from dependence, from our alienation from ourselves, and from a fear of abandonment. Intimacy does not flower in a climate of dependence, alienation, and fear. Intimacy flowers when two people, rooted in their self-hood, bring themselves equally, honestly, and wholly to one another.

Our dependence on loyalty to keep us together is like our dependence on ethics to make us good. In the same way that our deference to ethics undermines our ability to act from love, our loyalty undermines our ability to stay together out of love. We lose ourselves in ethics; we share ourselves in love. We bind ourselves in loyalty; we free ourselves in love. Ethics and loyalty (for whatever they may have to recommend them) are expressions of obligation, rightness, and adherence to tradition. Love is an expression of pleasure, delight, and joy.

Most relationships are held together by a mixture of love and obligation. It makes a sturdy adhesive, but a very messy one. When love and obligation are mixed, it's impossible to see their proportions. When we remove the sense of obligation from our relationships, we have nothing left holding our relationships together except love.

Our personal *neediness* causes us to stop listening to our own voice and to defer more consistently to the voice of Other. That Other-voice may be the voice of family, tradition, or culture, and that Other-voice may be our partner's voice. In our desperation to be attached, we may "disappear" into our partner. As romantic as that sounds, no matter who or what we disappear into, we're gone. These relationships become lopsided, and in them true intimacy—the communion of one Self with another—is impossible.

The solution lies in the restoration of peer-ness. In a true peer relationship, each person listens first to his own voice—the voice of Self, and then brings himself to his partner—Self-to-Self.

Fortunately, *neediness* is a choice. When we feel *needy* we rarely see the deliberateness in it (in fact its deliberateness may have faded into habit long ago). But a recognition of our own *neediness* is deliberate, and a recognition of our power to release ourselves from *neediness* is deliberate too.

Creating Purposeful Intensity

You may wish at times to convey a sense of intensity in order to get people enthused or concerned about something. *Need* and *try* convey intensity, but they introduce frustration along with it.

Here is a list of some other words that convey intensity. Read each word with an ear to the sort of intensity it conveys.

anxious	enthusiastic	intense	strong
aware	essential	urgent	beneficial

forceful	obligatory	vehement	committed
impassioned	oppressive	vigilant	devoted
important	passionate	vital	eager
indispensable	restrictive	zealous	excited
inspiring	strenuous		

We speak and write with greater accuracy when we consider the nuances of the language we use. Look, for example, at the use of *anxious* in instances where there is no anxiety.

Consider ‿

‿ I am *anxious* to start my new job.

which has a very different meaning from ‿

‿ I am *eager* to start my new job.

Either could be true. The first statement—I am *anxious*—implies that the speaker has misgivings (anxieties) about the new job. The second statement—I am *eager*—implies that the speaker is enthusiastic about the new job. If you claim to be *anxious* when you are *eager*, you create anxiety instead of eagerness.

Another mismatched pair, often used interchangeably, is *vigilant* and *aware*.

To be *vigilant* means to be watchful of danger—even sleeplessly watchful. To be *aware* means to be conscious, alert, informed, and knowledgeable. If I had reason to be *vigilant*, I would be *anxious* about it. But I am always *eager* to be more *aware*.

Below, I have categorized the words from the previous list, according to my own perception of their connotations.

Positive	Negative	Positive or Negative
aware	anxious	committed
beneficial	obligatory	essential
devoted	oppressive	forceful
eager	restrictive	impassioned
enthusiastic	urgent	indispensable

Positive	Negative	Positive or Negative
excited	vehement	strenuous
important	vigilant	strong
inspiring	zealous	vital
passionate		

You may disagree with my assessment of some of these words. Know that *your* assessment of these words is the one that matters, as my assessment is presented here only for comparison. Give some extra thought to the words on which your opinion differs from mine. If you are certain that your use of them does not create frustration, and instead conveys exactly what you mean, keep using them. Play with these words in different contexts to see how their connotations change.

Gracefully Receiving Statements of *Need*

Others will not change their habits of language just because you have—or even because you ask them to. Someone at some point will undoubtedly tell you what *you need*.

When others tell you what you *need*, you may tell them what you desire. There is no reason to shine much light on the moment. It can be as subtle as ∽

∽ Did you find everything you *need*?

∽ Yes, thank you; I found everything I was looking for.

or ∽

∽ You *need* to get a new car.

∽ I might want to buy a new one soon; I'll think about it.

Answer someone else's assertion of your *need* with a gentle assertion of your desire.

Self-Portrait: Phase Five

Every time you "do" instead of *trying*—every time you assert your desire instead of your *need*—you scrape your portrait clean.

When your layers of frustration are gone, you begin to figure things out—to own your problems and to solve them. The removal of your layers of frustration frees up a great deal of your mental and emotional energy. Figuring out what to do with that extra energy is a problem you'll have no trouble solving.

Paint the flower of your abundance. Scrape it off and notice the beauty of your new imprint.

CHAPTER SEVEN

Transcending Restriction: Can't & Have No Choice

Before we transcend restriction, let's examine our current relationship with it through an exercise called, "Find the Restriction."

1) Write or speak any positive affirmation, up to three words long, beginning with the pronoun *I*. (Examples: I am free. I am beautiful. I am kind.)

2) Figure out how each affirmation could be perceived as an expression of self-restriction.

3) Express applicable self-restrictions until you feel anxious.

Example One: I am free.

This appears on first glance to be the cure for self-restriction. But if I am free, am I not also completely responsible for all of my actions? If I am free, then I *have to* make all of my own choices. Free people *can't* just do what everybody else is doing; they *have no choice* but to figure things out for themselves.

Example Two: I am beautiful.

Beautiful people get a lot of attention. They *can't* tell who likes them for who they really are and who just likes them because they're beautiful. Beautiful people *have to* be vigilant, or other people will *try* to use them sexually.

Example Three: I am kind.

If I am kind, people will take advantage of me. They'll ask me to help and I'll *have no choice* but to help them or I won't be kind anymore.

The purpose of this exercise is not to demonstrate that freedom, beauty, and kindness are not all they're cracked up to be. It's meant to demonstrate a mode of thinking, usually far more subtle than the exaggerations found in these examples, that many of us slip into with little awareness. The purpose of this exercise is to help us to practice deliberately what is for many of us an unconscious habit, in hopes of recognizing this habit well enough to change it.

Do the exercise with an affirmation of your own. Exaggerate the restrictions you find. Invent restrictions to any extent that still feels logical (even if somewhat farcical). After two or three affirmations, it will become remarkably easy.

If we find restriction wherever we seek it, perhaps we create restriction by looking for it. And we *transcend* restriction by seeing through it.

Fixing Our Self-Talk

Eliminating *I Can't*

I can't is the voice of Other. We sacrifice our self-determination and deny our personal responsibility any time we so boldly claim restriction.

A claim of *I can't* is usually self-deceiving as well. Rarely do we actually meet obstacles that prevent us completely from doing what we'd like. When we habitually claim we *can't*, we experience the stuckness of self-limitation, and that stuckness is compounded by the gooey trap of our self-deception. Because it is our unconscious habit to claim the restriction of *I can't*, we don't pause to consider the validity of that claim, and our lies magnify our limitations time and again.

Recall ⌒

⌒ *I can't* get to the gym after work.

If at any time it was your intention to go to the gym, it would benefit you to acknowledge that you have been choosing to do other things *instead* of going to the gym. With *I can't*, we deny our self-determination, implying that an Unseen Oppressor keeps us from the gym,

80

and we inadvertently lie about it to ourselves and others. When departing from a point like this one, we are not very likely to get where we're headed. It is both more optimistic and more accurate to say ⌐

⌐ I haven't been getting to the gym after work.

This implies that there is hope for the future, leaving the door open for a time when you *can*. And, though it does not go out of its way to express self-determination, at least it does not invite the Unseen Oppressor in to deny it for you. If in this scenario you wish to re-commit yourself to going to the gym, you can be clear and specific about your intention with something like ⌐

⌐ I'm going to the gym three times a week now.

When I decided to eliminate *I can't* from my vocabulary, the toughest construction for me to change was ⌐

⌐ *I can't* remember…

I felt the oppression of *I can't* even when I said it in this seemingly harmless way, so I wanted to change my habit. After a fair amount of verbal stumbling, I reshaped my desire to remember into ⌐

⌐ I'm not remembering…

and then improved it twice more from ⌐

⌐ I'm not remembering yet…

to ⌐

⌐ I'm about to remember…

We also say *I can't* to proclaim our dependence, as in ⌐

⌐ *I can't* live without my coffee in the morning.

But we don't benefit from affirming our addiction in this statement. It is also, of course, not true that we would die without our morning coffee. I admit this is a tough one. We could state this more positively as ⌐

⌐ I love how coffee makes me feel in the morning!

But that might be more enthusiasm than some of us are likely to muster *before* we have that first cup. Perhaps we can quietly sip our joe until we feel equal to the day. Sometimes the best way to avoid the language of restriction is to keep quiet.

Eliminating Opposition

To oppose something requires an investment of energy into whatever it is we strive to oppose. You multiply your experience of restriction and risk the creation of an opposite-same any time you invest your energies in opposition.

Consider the double-negative *can't* ⌣

⌣ I *don't* see why I *can't* meet you there later.

You mean for this to be a positive statement. But you've stated it as if someone had tossed up the obstacle that it *would* be a problem for you to meet, and as if you've *had to* overcome that obstacle. By giving voice to your opposition, you magnify your restriction. Instead you can remove the opposition with ⌣

⌣ I can meet you there later.

Consider also ⌣

⌣ I *can't* see why *not.*

This implies that you looked thoroughly for any obstacles before you felt comfortable enough to commit to an affirmative response. That's an emotionally taxing habit of language. You look to the four corners of the room to see that the coast is clear when all you mean to say is ⌣

⌣ Okay.

Similarly, when you begin a question with *can't,* you start off with the inference that you have been restricted—that you have obstacles to overcome, as in ⌣

⌣ *Can't I* reschedule for tomorrow?

Here we react to someone having given us some trouble about scheduling an appointment. We fuel the discord if we acknowledge it with a resistant reaction. Instead, de-escalate the moment with ⌒

⌒ Can I reschedule for tomorrow?

Or if there is a prescriptive grammarian nearby, you might even say ⌒

⌒ *May* I reschedule for tomorrow?

Eliminating *I Have No Choice*

Implicit in the *I have no choice* stance is the notion that we are in some way forced to act as we do. With it, we imply that someone or something oppresses us. This Unseen Oppressor frees us (ironically) to disappear from any situation. In our place, the Unseen Oppressor either keeps us from doing as we wish or bullies people for us, taking the heat for us at the same time.

We say that we *have no choice* when we want to claim powerlessness. In truth, our power is not diminished simply because we fail to claim it. We affirm the lie of our powerlessness—and create the experience of restriction—every time we claim to *have no choice.*

Your choices are numerous. You may not feel as though some of your choices are very attractive, but it is remarkably freeing to acknowledge that you *have* other choices.

We sometimes claim we *have no choice* in order to disguise our self-indulgences. Claiming we *have no choice* puts us (or so we imagine) above criticism.

Consider ⌒

⌒ *I have no choice* but to get a massage when my neck is aching.

We don't want anyone to think we pay for pleasure. But if we really believe that a massage is too indulgent, we won't get one. You'll enjoy your indulgences more if you speak honestly about them. You could take responsibility for your actions and happily admit your self-indulgence with ⌒

⌣ I really enjoy the massages I've been getting lately.

When we claim to *have no choice*, we don't even consider whether self-indulgence is justifiable in our situation, rushing directly to the notion that we don't even have the *choice* to be self-indulgent. But it's a lie; we *do* have a choice.

We even bring the self-deceptive notion that we *have no choice* into our parenting, as we invite the Unseen Oppressor to discipline our children, with ⌣

⌣ *I have no choice* but to ground you for skipping school.

Of course we have a choice. We're choosing to enforce a consequence with our child rather than letting her endanger her future by skipping school. Why are we not happy to be consistent, involved parents? We can take credit for our actions instead and say ⌣

⌣ I want you to realize the magnitude of what you did, so I'm grounding you for skipping school.

Here the parent stays present and lovingly enforces a reasonable consequence with his child.

Beneath Language

As you learn to talk to yourself without the language of restriction, you begin to feel less restricted. But it is naïve to assume that a change in linguistic habits alone will instantly bring you complete freedom from feelings of restriction. It is quite possible to change your language habits without immediately changing what lies beneath them.

As you begin to incorporate alternatives to *I can't* and *I have no choice*, you may feel at times that you are lying to yourself. In practice, eliminating feelings of restriction is not quite as simple as "*saying* you can" until you "*feel* you can." The elimination of self-oppressing speech is a vital step toward eliminating experiences of self-oppression; but it is *one* step. In some instances you'll simply correct yourself by not saying *I can't* when you *can*. But you may also wish to avoid saying you *can't* when perhaps you legitimately *are* in some way restricted, in order to lessen your experience of restriction.

Consider this scenario: You are a teacher in a classroom. Your lesson is going well and you have the attention of your students. Suddenly a fight breaks out. Your first anxious thought is, *"I can't* control my students!"* While there is a fair amount of truth to the notion that we *can't* control other people, it is a notion that creates anxiety. Equally true, and far more freeing, is the thought, *"What do I want* to do in this situation?"* In the panic of your other-focussed *"I can't,"* you put all of your attention on the problem—and on your inability to solve it. With "What do I want?" you retain enough of your*self* to devise a satisfying solution.

Your first aim in eliminating the language of restriction is to decrease your *false* sense of restriction. If you stop claiming restriction where there is none, you free yourself to see opportunity where you have not seen it before.

Your second aim in avoiding the language of restriction is to illuminate and explore your *feelings* of restriction. What you gain by avoiding the language of restriction in instances where you really *do* feel restricted is, first, a clearer awareness of what's really happening in those situations; second, a moment to consider whether your feelings of restriction are real or imagined; and third, an opportunity to find the elements of freedom hiding in any experience of restriction.

Gracefully Receiving Statements of Restriction

It is rare that anyone will tell you that you *have no choice* in order to limit your choices. More often, others will tell you that you *have no choice* when they see you faced with difficulty.

⌐ You really *had no choice* but to leave your job.

When people tell you that you *have no choice*, their intention is usually to validate the stickiness of your situation.

When others imply that there is only one choice for you, take the opportunity to demonstrate that you can see more choices than the obvious one—even if your intention is not to choose any of the other options. Such occasions provide a chance for you to convey self-determination.

Talking to Others

We are not likely to say anything as obviously restricting as ⌒

⌒ *You can't* cross this line.

We're far more likely to restrict others in less direct ways. We restrict others by pointing out ways in which we perceive them to be limited, as in ⌒

⌒ *You can't* make it as a rock star.

But there are many other ways in which we use the phrase *you can't* that seem quite harmless. They are not. The most damaging consequence of our telling others that they *can't* is that we attack their sense of entitlement.

How many times will you hear *you can't* in any context before you begin to internalize its message?

⌒ *You can't* be serious.

⌒ *You can't* sign up for this class.

⌒ *You can't* have a snack before dinner.

⌒ *You can't* teach an old dog new tricks.

These are the sorts of messages we hear and say every day.

Restriction Creates Entitlement Issues

When we are told that we *can't* or we *have no choice*, that assertion comes as a direct threat to our sense of entitlement. If we buy into the notion that we are powerless, we will shape our lives to either reflect or oppose that notion.

Here's how entitlement works. The most successful people in the world (and we'll define success in a moment) are not necessarily the smartest, hardest working, or most gifted. The most successful people in the world are those who believe they are entitled to succeed.

While a sense of entitlement can take a wide variety of forms, we'll consider four types. The Obverse sense of entitlement (really a sense of *non*-entitlement), the Defiant sense of entitlement, and the Petulant sense of entitlement create various difficulties for us. The fourth type—the Individual sense of entitlement—creates satisfying, meaningful success.

A consequence of our internalizing the message *you can't* is that we come to feel undeserving, and we suffer the repercussions of an Obverse sense of entitlement. We may carry a defeatist stance into our pursuits, even if we do not outwardly reveal ourselves as people who struggle with anything of the sort. Those with an Obverse sense of entitlement don't expect much (though they may tell themselves and others that they do), so they don't get much. With an Obverse sense of entitlement, we repeat the restrictions we've had imposed on us. We integrate the notions that we *can't* and that we *have no choice*.

Those with an Obverse sense of entitlement undervalue their own accomplishments, reasoning that anything they could accomplish *must* not be much of an accomplishment at all. Because of their distorted view of their accomplishments, they have an equally distorted view of how they fit into the world. Their definition of success is unclear, and they sense that success lurks somewhere out of their reach. They either agree with or oppose the notion that they belong in the underachiever group, but in either case, they put a fair amount of energy into the critical assessment of their achievements.

People with an Obverse sense of entitlement have an unclear perception of how others restrict them, but they are fairly certain that they do. And because they have an underdeveloped sense of Self, they don't know what they want.

The Obverse sense of entitlement is often the springboard for the next two senses of entitlement. In our *opposition* to the notion that we are ineffective and undeserving, we may create for ourselves an "opposite-same," in which we become Defiant or Petulant.

Those with a Defiant sense of entitlement see the world as a challenge. In Opposition Consciousness, they set out to prove their *can't-sayers* wrong.

Their experience of opposition can be an effective fuel for some visible show of success. If a person comes into the world with no advantages, he might see the world as a set of obstacles to overcome, and he may in fact overcome them. But his position is backward-looking, as he runs from his past with as much energy as he uses to move toward his future. He may find some satisfaction in having gotten away from whatever he's left behind, but what he moves toward is usually a traditional, conventionally defined success. For the person with a Defiant sense of entitlement, success is made of money, possessions, and beautiful people. He measures his success by the opinions (real or imagined) of others. There is no *personal* satisfaction for him because his definition of success does not come from himself.

Someone with a Defiant sense of entitlement may see himself as a recovered victim, but he is a victim nonetheless. He may tell us that he has earned everything he's got, that nothing's been handed to him, or that he's never played on a level playing field. But he does himself no favors by describing his life as a victory over victimization; he defines himself almost entirely in terms of what he opposes.

The Petulant sense of entitlement is found in the person who will ask for (or take) whatever she wants, no matter who else might be put out. She makes no distinction between her reactive whims and her authentic desires because she is not deeply self-reflective. Her sense of what constitutes success is undefined; she is only sure that she wants what others will envy. In part, it is her impersonal sense of what she wants that keeps her from ever feeling personally satisfied. Consequently, the most common expression of the Petulant sense of entitlement is what seems like nothing more than an exercise of power to test that the power still exists. She wants to see that all of the obstacles she has placed herself in opposition to are still under her control.

The person with a Petulant sense of entitlement invests urgency into all that she does, and she sees anything you do that might slow her down as an attempt to restrict her. She has no idea what a powerful role opposition plays in her life.

The person with a Petulant sense of entitlement restricts others, often overtly. She is the person who says ◠

◠ I want that *now*, whether you're finished or not.

She bullies others because she fears that no one will agree with her. But if she allowed herself a moment of self-reflection, she would find that no amount of getting what she wants *now* is as satisfying as working out an agreement. The person with a Petulant sense of entitlement appears "selfish," but in reality it is her lack of connection with her Self that motivates her desperate grabs for power.

It could all go differently if she had an Individual sense of entitlement. What if she said ◠

◠ When will you be finished? I'm eager to get started.

Once we transcend obligation we no longer do what we think we *should*. Once we transcend frustration we no longer *try* to get what we think we *need*. Once we transcend restriction, we no longer believe that we *can't*, or that there is any situation in which we *have no choice*. When the voices of obligation, frustration, and restriction are gone, we hear our own desires and satisfy them. If we desire to succeed by our own definition of success, we do. This is the Individual sense of entitlement.

Whatever situation you were born into, no matter how old you are, it is never too late to develop an Individual sense of entitlement. As you notice your own entitlement issues—as you subjugate yourself to other people or as you watch yourself step on their desires—you can cultivate an awareness of your emotions connected with those experiences. (In our experience of those emotions we may glimpse the inner scar that disfigured our sense of entitlement in the first place.) That awareness and your willingness to experience your emotions will move you, little by little, toward an Individual sense of entitlement.

With an Individual sense of entitlement, you define success personally. You no longer *need* the approval of others, and you feel no obligation to conform. You experience a greater freedom of thought, which leads to freedom of attitude and action. You have no sense of victimization because you no longer speak its language. You have no self-imposed limits, and you do not perceive anyone else's action as a threat to your sense of entitlement. With an Individual sense of entitlement, you feel that everything you desire is within reach.

Self-Portrait: Phase Six

Light returns when you scrape away your layers of restriction. Your vision clears and you see possibility wherever you look.

With your layers of obligation, frustration, and restriction scraped away, you hear your own desires. You figure out what *you* want to do. You solve your own problems. And you see more choices than you ever have before.

Scrape your canvas down to its purest, least affected form. Freeing yourself from layers of self-oppression is a way of starting over.

Dip your brush in the brightest color on your palette. Paint a symbol of your purpose. Scrape it off and admire the indelible imprint it adds to your self-portrait.

Breathe

I wish I could tell you it was going to be easy to eliminate the language of self-oppression from your life. It will probably take a few weeks of verbal stumbling followed by several more months of experimentation and refinement before you completely eliminate should, have to, must, ought to, need, try, can't *and* have no choice *from your vocabulary.*

While some of the benefits of using self-empowering speech are immediate, the truly transformative power of this endeavor occurs over a period of months—even years. Don't think of the elimination of self-oppressing speech as the means to an end. It is an end in itself.

If you get to a point where you feel frustrated, stop trying. *Instead, look back over how far you've come. If you've made progress—if you've been asking yourself about your desires and indulging them, if you've felt more abundant, less deprived, if you've begun to feel more free and peaceful and powerful—stick with it. I promise you it's worth it.*

PART FOUR

The World's Opinion

"It is easy in the world to live after the world's opinion; it is easy in
solitude to live after our own; but the great man is he who in the midst
of the crowd keeps with perfect sweetness the independence of solitude."
—Ralph Waldo Emerson

CHAPTER EIGHT

Self-Regard

The notion of *Self* has perhaps as many connotations, both negative and positive, as the notion of God. We refer to ourselves casually (I made that my*self*—) and in those instances we use the term *self* with little emphasis or importance. It's when we use *self* as a prefix, that the language with which we refer to the Self reveals our self-regard.

Look at some of the words we attach to the prefix *self*. We lend the Self to self-absorption, self-righteousness, self-aggrandizement, and self-loathing. Admittedly, we also lend it to more complimentary terms like self-possession, self-confidence, and self-reliance. But our wariness toward the Self is evident in awkward coinages like selfish-in-a-good-way. We wince at the idea that the Self might merit indulgence, while we believe that it benefits immeasurably from discipline.

We sometimes make references to the Self that appear neutral. More often than not we are unkind in our assumptions about the Self in those instances. For example, while we may admire self-initiative, self-enrichment is permissible at best, and only as long as no one is inconvenienced. We look carefully at context before judging someone's self-concern. Self-focus sounds like conceit. Self-amusement is childish. Self-promotion is shameful. Self-adulation, self-celebration and self-reverence are in some circles all but unforgivable. Our reaction to these words is largely automatic, and our habitual bashing of the Self distorts our sense of self-worth.

No matter how much self-respect we think we have, if we refer to the Self with unflattering language, we don't respect ourselves as much as we think we do.

Self as Suspect

Our collective concept of Self has passed through countless hands on its way to us. Throughout history, people all over the world have looked over the fence to see what others were doing, found it excessive, and crushed them for it.

Our long history of destroying others because of their self-expression has deformed our own sense of Self. We seem to believe that we *must* be kept under control—as if left unrestrained, we are likely to injure or corrupt anyone with whom we come into contact.

This suspicion of Self creates vigilance, and our vigilance causes us to monitor ourselves. We don't want to get too smug, so we criticize ourselves. We don't want to do anything corrupt, so we discipline ourselves. We believe that our vigilance is helpful, but it's not. It only serves to remind us of the more distasteful acts of which human beings have proven themselves capable.

Our vigilance of human nature (our *own* nature) may be easier to recognize when it's directed toward others. We may believe that we *have to* be vigilant of people in power, even in situations where we would never actually challenge their authority. This sort of vigilance nearly always takes voice as criticism. We may be critical of members of our government, of big business, of liberals or conservatives, or of powerful people in general. And we may half believe that if we didn't keep a close eye on them, they'd misuse us even more egregiously than they do now. Unfortunately, all of this vigilance of other people is really an act of self-oppression. It commandeers our mental and emotional energy, but it influences, disciplines, and regulates no one.

The cure for vigilance is trust. If we hold a basic trust of the Self (a basic trust of ourselves) we eventually come to the more satisfying attitude of acceptance. But it's important to realize that our new trust will not do the job we meant to do with our old vigilance. If we once entertained the fantasy that our vigilance alone somehow kept wrong-doers from doing wrong, our trust will do nothing to further that misguided agenda. In practice, our vigilant monitoring of people in power does not affect them in any way. What *does* affect them is action. If we remain peacefully aware of the deeds of the powerful people with whom we disagree, we can *act*—with our votes, our voices, our purchasing power, and our own often untapped political power—to prevent or counteract their misdeeds.

Trusting ourselves is difficult for many of us. Even if you see yourself as someone who consistently makes wise, temperate, solid decisions, you may still harbor a deep suspicion of the Self. If, as a result, you speak of the Self with suspicion, you'll obligate, frustrate, and restrict yourself in ways that severely limit your potential.

Selflessness

The language of self-oppression—*I should, I have to, I must, I ought to, I need, I try, I can't,* and *I have no choice*—is also the language of selflessness.

Think back to the section in Chapter Six on *need*iness in romantic relationships. In his desire for intimacy, the *needy* lover dissolved into his partner. In his over-focus on the object of his affection, he sacrificed him*self*. He sacrificed himself with the best intentions, but his sacrifice left him with far less of himself to share. But intense dependence on another person is only *one* way in which we lose our*selves*.

We hide ourselves in self-righteousness when we claim obligation to do what's *right* by some impersonal ethical standard. In our self-righteousness we de-personalize personal decisions. We act not on our own desires, but on what we assume is appropriate. But where is the Self in a decision based on what is appropriate? With our own values set aside in favor of ethics, we lose our*selves*.

We sometimes "give ourselves away" in the guise of helping others. We take pride in our willingness to sacrifice for others, and others admire us for our selflessness. But what sort of intention lies behind our sacrifice? If we help because we *should*, we help out of obligation. If we help because we believe others *need* us, we magnify their dependence. If we help because we *have no choice*, we do not act from love no matter how loving a gesture we appear to make.

We sometimes "put ourselves aside" (a euphemism for losing ourselves completely, though only for a set period of time). I used to read books and articles with someone else's problems in mind. I was so focussed on other people that my own problems didn't exist for me. I'd read with thoughts like, "*I have to* tell so-and-so about this; it's all about *her* situation"—when in reality the ideas applied as much to me as they did to anyone else. Where was *I* in that equation? I was standing outside the perimeter of my own life, diagnosing my friends and acquaintances, sacrificing myself for them. But they gained no more from my sacrifice than I did. My sacrifice was as valuable as my lopping off a finger so that others may have a severed finger at their disposal.

While selflessness is traditionally thought of as an admirable quality, its definition in this book is expanded to include the unfortunate pattern of giving ourselves away by unconscious habit—losing Self to no one's benefit. As I have re-defined selflessness in a rather unflattering way, I want to offer an antidote to it. Most obviously, perhaps, the opposite of selflessness is selfishness. But the antidote to accidental selflessness is not to run to it's opposite; it is to figure out what you desire for your *Self*. Do you desire to lose yourself in service or do you desire to withhold your services completely—or does your desire lead you toward a satisfying middle ground?

The Fallacy of Sacrificial Giving

Perhaps the best known and most admired giver in our collective memory is Mother Teresa, the Catholic nun who spent fifty years in Calcutta taking care of the poor and sick. At a glance her life appears to be one of unrelieved sacrifice. We admire her for her sacrifice because we have been taught that sacrifice is admirable. But if our admiration stops at her sacrifice, we have misunderstood the true nature of her giving.

Sacrifice takes many different forms. A girl donates a kidney to her brother, sacrificing a part of her body to save her brother's life. A woman sacrifices her career to raise her children. A man sacrifices his car to pay his rent. A gang member sacrifices his freedom to murder the guy who insulted his cousin. A terrorist flies an airplane into a tower, sacrificing his own life to further his political agenda.

Sacrifice is not inherently noble.

It was not sacrifice that inspired Mother Teresa; it was love. Mother Teresa could not have served as she did for so long and in such difficult conditions if she was not renewed by the service she provided. She said, "It is not how much we give, but how much love we put in the giving." She saw service to others as an opportunity to express love, not sacrifice.

We romanticize sacrifice. When we romanticize our *own* sacrifice, we miss a great deal of the satisfaction of giving. The high value we place on sacrifice may even lead us to find our giving deficient when it is not adequately sacrificial.

Consider this pair: the person in the trenches, giving aid and comfort to directly alleviate the suffering of another—and the person in an executive suite making money to support the work of a thousand people giving aid and comfort. Who gives the better gift?

The gift of the person raising money to support a mass of people giving comfort is neither better nor worse than the gift of the person giving front-line care. Both gifts are valuable; in fact, neither giver would accomplish as much without the other. Let's assume that for all practical purposes, their gifts are equally valuable.

Now let's look at the nature of each giver's giving. Each gives out of either love or sacrifice. But the gift itself is neither tarnished nor brightened by the nature of the giving. It is the *giver* who is most directly affected by her spirit of love or sacrifice.

If you give sacrificially, you experience sacrifice in your giving; if you give lovingly, you experience love in your giving. Language shapes our experiences by framing them with elements of story—by telling us something about our experiences as we experience them. You have the choice of telling yourself that you are giving until it hurts, or that you are giving as an indulgence of your loving desire to give.

By this reasoning, the front-line bringer of comfort may experience joy along with dysentery, while the person in the executive suite may swallow misery with her caviar. We choose to be either bound or liberated by our giving based on the intention behind it—and that intention is shaped by the stories we tell ourselves about it.

In much the same way that we trust obligation to bind us to our tasks, we trust sacrifice to ensure our goodness. But it doesn't. If we wish to experience our goodness through giving, we'll experience that goodness through the indulgence of our desire to give—not through fulfilling an obligation to give.

Over time, the stance from which we give influences our effectiveness. Sacrificial giving depletes us. It encourages us to give up part of ourselves, presumably because it is admirable to do so. Sacrifice is encouraged by the voice of Other and it compels us to great acts of courage and generosity. But chasing after the assumed wishes of countless others is exhausting. When we *do-what's-right-because-it's-right*, we fail to trust that it's love that ultimately leads us to our most fulfilling service to others.

Giving from love renews us. It inspires us to give because we value giving, and because we love both the gift and the recipient of that gift. Giving from love leads us to give what we deeply desire to give, with the result that we are deeply satisfied by each act of giving—and that we are energized to give again and again.

Our disparaging references to Self and our misguided admiration of selflessness and sacrifice place us in opposition to the very notion of the Self, setting us up to create against ourselves. Unless we learn to refer to ourselves with the reverence we deserve, we will not reclaim Self. We do not let ourselves become what we scorn.

Self-Portrait: Phase Seven

At some point in your life, you have expressed suspicion of the Self, slipped into selflessness, or given sacrificially. These actions have made you anxious. They have made you afraid to see yourself clearly.

Pick up your scraper and scrape off your fear. What you find beneath the layers may not be pretty, but you're not stuck with it.

Paint your way into a new picture of Self. If you want to be the sun, the moon, or a star, paint it now. Add any figure you wish in any color you love. Scrape it off, and note how the imprint has changed. Paint it again. Then scrape it to its purest, least affected form.

CHAPTER NINE

The Dissolving Self

Original Learning: Dissolving into Family

Our deference to the voice of Other is an old habit. We learn it in our families.

We come into this world helpless. From that point on, people help us. They feed us and cuddle us and they teach us right from wrong. We listen to them because we're wired to take instruction from the people who feed and cuddle us.

We get our first sense of who we are from how we are treated by our parents. They do their best for us—they *try* hard to do everything they *should*. But I've learned something very important about parents since becoming one: We don't know what we're doing.

And neither did our parents. They were limited by their experience, intelligence, and creativity; by their education, both formal and informal; by their experience of their own parents; perhaps by tradition; or by the conventional parenting advice of their generation.

It is under the supervision of these improbable guides that we assemble identities to fit into our families. We start before we are conscious, and we have no idea what we're doing. By adolescence we've taken on layers of beliefs, traits, and behaviors for conformity, safety, or even survival within the family.

Consider this example of what our families give us to work with: We get most of our early information about love and romantic relationships from our parents, grandparents, and other older family members. While they might attempt to be objective with us, they have an agenda: Our first lessons about love come from people whose primary concern for us is that we don't get hurt. As a result, much of what we are taught about love early on comes in the form of warnings. After all, men are after only one thing, right?

Our families want to ensure our safety and well-being. The wisdom they impart may be helpful information at the time, but it is not (and is probably not meant to be) timeless wisdom for us to believe without question forever. Unfortunately, no one comes back and tells us, "By the way, that thing I told you when you were ten was only supposed to apply until you were seventeen."

As children we learn constantly. We learn from how we are treated—we learn by observation—from deliberate teaching—from the media—we often learn from mixed messages. Unfortunately, much of what we learn slips in beneath consciousness. (It was true when we were children and it happens even now.) As a consequence, we may still believe what someone taught us when we were three. We may even believe some notion gleaned from something we *misunderstood* when we were three.

Stubborn Layers

Some of our most solid "beliefs" are those that came to us as indoctrinations—ideas deliberately instilled in us through persistent or repetitious teaching. They are not necessarily misinformation, as someone might securely fix a perfectly sound notion in our head. But indoctrinations are not personal, so they are not really *our* beliefs. If we recite indoctrinations as if they are our own truths, or if we act on our indoctrinations automatically, we forgo opportunities to ask ourselves about our own thoughts and opinions—our own values, desires, or beliefs.

Indoctrinations look like these:

- Rich people are snobs.
- It's a sin to waste.
- If you want something, you've got to earn it.
- Your friends will leave you, but you'll always have your family.

Each indoctrination is as likely to be true or untrue as another. But whatever wisdom our indoctrinations may hold, our unquestioning belief in them insults our intelligence.

Loyalty to indoctrination keeps us dissolved into our original families. We remain limbs of the family body until we see ourselves as individuals. Ideally, when we become adults and experience something counter to what our families taught us, we re-evaluate what is true and create our own beliefs. But getting rid of indoctrinations is like throwing out live mice; they like to run back inside.

Notice your indoctrinations and decide what role, if any, you want them to play in your life. But avoid defiance of your indoctrinations. If you snap to an opposite—opposing your indoctrinations under the assumption that they could be of no possible use to you—you will create an opposite-same that will not satisfy you. When you become aware of your indoctrinations, ask yourself how you want to deal with them. Ask yourself whether they are true, whether they are loving, whether they are relevant, and whether you want to continue believing them. There are no wrong answers to your self-referential questions.

Accidental Identities

In our original families we form identities. These identities are made up primarily of character traits and physical characteristics. We come to see ourselves and others as combinations of ⌒

- ⌒ our thoughts, beliefs, values, memories, and emotions
- ⌒ our desires, preferences, and world-view
- ⌒ our physical characteristics
- ⌒ our personality traits
- ⌒ our personal and cultural associations
- ⌒ our geographical and social positions in the world
- ⌒ our actions

Since we form our identities as children, we do so with little consciousness. We put on the elements of identity as they begin to fit. Eventually we become conscious enough to contemplate who we are, and at that point we begin to define ourselves more or less as collections of these traits.

While identity aids socialization, no one is merely a collection of traits, so our accidental identities—those we put on unconsciously and leave unquestioned—ultimately obscure who we really are. When we live beneath layers of identity we live as pseudo-selves.

At some point in our development we learn to "manage" our layers of identity in order to become who we think we want to be. As a pre-teen I wanted to be tall, thin, and rich. I wasn't, so I took on other identifications that helped me to be valuable in hopes that someone would admire me and choose me as a friend. I took on layers and "managed" them in ways that I thought would help me. At age ten I went from "sulky" to "funny." At eleven I went from "tough" to "nice." At thirteen I went from "smart-alecky" to "smart." With the real me tucked safely beneath those layers—even those layers I managed so constructively—I was operating as a pseudo-self.

Throughout our lives, we fall back on identity to define ourselves. Each time we notice that we are identifying ourselves by an external characteristic, we can take a moment to acknowledge that nothing external by which we identify ourselves is a permanent, unalterable part of us. Until we learn to recognize our external identifications, we remain locked into identities that help us dissolve.

The Safety of Lies

We learn to lie to ourselves and to others in our families. By adulthood, we may no longer trust that we know the truth when we hear it. When we were children we learned to be quiet when we wanted to talk, to sleep when we weren't tired, and to say that everything was okay when it wasn't. We fail to trust ourselves now because our relationship with the truth was once so nonsensical.

Opposite-Same: Dissolving into Others

With the voice of Other fixed in our heads, we meet people. When we discover anything from comfortable common ground to inexplicably compelling attraction, we attach.

We form close relationships throughout our lives. When we bring ourselves equally and openly to each other in these close relationships, we form intimate relationships. This sounds like a simple and natural progression, but it isn't. The dissolution we learn in our original families puts us at a marked disadvantage when forming relationships outside of the family.

Intimate relationships—the communion of two people in their purest, least affected state—are peer relationships. But the degree to which either of the participants in an apparently intimate relationship sees him or herself as *individual* determines the extent to which either is capable of peer relationship.

Family Systems theorists claim that when we leave our original families we tend to find people who have differentiated from their original families as much (or as little) as we have. (Self-differentiation, also known as individuation, is the process of reclaiming Self.) If we are relatively *un*differentiated, we continue to repeat the patterns of our original learning (often as opposite-sames) and we intuitively find people to repeat them with us.

Individuation challenges us to look at the imbalances in our would-be peer relationships. As peer-ness does not exist before individuation, the relationships we form prior to our reclamation of Self are invariably mis-shaped by our lack of it.

Imitation Intimacy

If we've been though enough therapy, spiritual study, or recovery programs (or if we are women), we probably speak openly of our triumphs and tragedies, and for it, we think of ourselves as intimate. But in close relationships where we still depend upon others for our voice, we merely imitate intimacy.

If we go looking in our relationships for advice or validation we ask others to be our voice. If in our relationships we seek out people who *want* our advice or validation, we become for them the voice of Other. Though in some relationships we may take turns being the voice and the voiceless, even a reciprocal imbalance makes true peer-ness—and true intimacy—impossible.

The lies we learn to tell ourselves in our original families train us for the lies of imitation intimacy. Telling ourselves that we are "intimate enough" mimics our original learning that we *should* pretend that everything is okay. But true intimacy requires revealing the Self—it requires scraping away as much identity as possible. If our original learning still has us dissolving into one another, we do not retain enough presence to do any meaningful revealing. Even if we speak the language of intimacy, until we clear away our internalized voices and listen consistently to our *own* voice, we are not *Self*-conscious enough to be truly intimate with anyone. We can be interdependent, enmeshed, or codependent, but before individuation, that's as close to intimacy as we get.

Close, Non-Sexual Relationships

Before individuation we bring ourselves to others with the desire to connect. In our desire to connect, we weave ourselves into the stories, ideas, and emotions of others. In practice, these connections can feel very satisfying. If we enjoy talking and listening—if we find companionship and opportunity in these connections—we can be content in these relationships for quite some time. We don't miss what we don't know we're missing.

I had always thought of myself as an "automatic intimate." I thought that superficial acquaintanceships were a waste of time, and I rarely had any difficulty getting people to follow me into more meaningful discussions. I found most often that people were relieved to talk about something meaningful, so I was spurred on by my positive reception. I told myself that I was an inherently intimate person because I was a deep talker. It was decades before I learned that deep talk is not necessarily intimacy.

As with many deep talkers, I longed to connect with people. I wanted to see myself as valuable, and for me that meant helping. Since I couldn't help with the weather or the price of bread, I initiated personal conversations. I didn't see at the time that I was feeding the *neediness* in other people. I was looking for some small wound that I could soothe with my insight or advice.

I was playing out an opposite-same. As a child I'd felt undervalued. I somehow got the message (perhaps from something I misunderstood when I was three) that I was useless. So, beginning at around age 7, I opposed the notion that I was useless, and in Opposition Consciousness I set myself up as an insightful, wound-soothing advice giver. In this new guise I helped kids with their problems—from the little girl who was picked on for her bucked teeth to the boy who was laughed at for not knowing an answer in class—I was there with insightful, wound-soothing advice. It looked from a distance like I'd fixed my problem of feeling useless. But I hadn't.

At the root of my feeling useless was the fear that others wouldn't love me unless I was useful. I'd felt in my family that I was chasing after love, and I created a situation outside of my family in which I did the same thing. In my creation of an *opposite*, I went from useless to indispensable, but with the *same* result—I chased after people in the desperate hope that they would love me. A return to my*self* (admittedly difficult at age seven) would have made possible some satisfaction of my desire to feel loved. Instead I played out a very functional looking opposite-same, and I did it for over thirty years.

I brought a strong pseudo-self (one buried beneath layers of identification with helpfulness and personal worth) to all of my close relationships. And while I had the best of intentions, my desperate chase after the love of others left me with no more than a remarkably convincing imitation of intimacy to offer.

Romantic Relationships

I believe that in romantic attraction, it is the Self that draws us in. We peek beneath the layers, if only for a moment, and we connect Self-to-Self.

Then we start thinking. We don't know how to be our*selves*, so we look for elements of identity to cling to. We find characteristics in the other person that please us. But when we leave that first moment of Self-to-Self attraction and begin to construct relationships based upon external identity, these attractive, but ultimately superficial characteristics may eventually begin to displease us.

We gravitate toward someone calm and relaxed only to end up disappointed with his lack of initiative. We are thrilled to find someone who always knows what she wants only to discover how opinionated she is. We go out of our way to find someone high-energy only to wake up next to a motor-mouth with the metabolism of a flea. We no longer see the Self that initially attracted us, and we maintain only enough vision to find his or her actions and characteristics lacking.

When mates disappoint us, we have choices to make, and we make those choices based on the extent to which we are individuated. If we are relatively non-individuated (poised to dissolve into our lover as we dissolved into our families), we may selflessly cater to the whims of our lover, we may cling to loved ones in desperate devotion, or we may bring an even more overtly dysfunctional *need*iness to our relationship with a cycle of physical or emotional abuse—all in order to stay connected. We do these things in opposition to the notion that our relationships are coming apart, so they function at best as opposite-sames, keeping us together, but failing to address the root causes of our relationship problems. But most tragically of all, when we dissolve into others, we turn away from ourselves. And when we turn away from ourselves, we unconsciously encourage others to turn away from us also.

Ironically, it is often when we feel most separate from our mate, that we are in fact most dissolved *into* our mate. (If we chase after our mate's approval we may feel separate when we don't get it. But the chase for approval is itself an act of dissolving.) The cure for this dissolution is not further focus on either what we wish to oppose in our mate or even what we find acceptable. The cure is to clarify who we are in the midst of these difficult moments—to evaluate the current situation, and to figure out how to repaint ourselves as we *desire* to be. Only then can we invite others to re-imagine themselves. We can appeal to *their* idea of who *they* want to be. Once we regain our own sense of Self our message to our mate is not, "Go back to being the way you were when I still liked you," but, "Be the way you are when you like yourself best."

Retaining a solid sense of who we are is challenging in even the most fulfilling relationships. Our mate pushes one of our buttons and we suddenly feel adolescent. If we don't notice our emotions in those moments and soothe ourselves as best we can, we are likely to lose our grip on whatever Self we have reclaimed and to slip into Opposition Consciousness. But if we learn to recognize our feelings of opposition, these crisis moments may provide our most promising opportunities to reconnect with ourselves.

We lose and reclaim ourselves countless times within the course of a relationship. Learning to reclaim ourselves helps us spend less time thinking about what's wrong with other people and more time being who *we* want to be.

Hiding the Self

Because of our long-held suspicion of the Self, we sometimes go to great lengths to hide it. We hide the Self beneath the pseudo-self. And we hide the Self in relationships that imitate intimacy.

We often foster the imitation intimacies of the pseudo-self because we don't know any better. But there may be more intuition at work here than ignorance. I believe we foster the imitation intimacy of the pseudo-self because we are deeply afraid of revealing our authentic Self to others. If the pseudo-self is found lacking, our wound is superficial. But we fear that if we present an authentic Self to others, we will be discovered as authentically inadequate. We avoid reclaiming Self because we know intuitively that the result will be intimacy, along with its imbedded threat of our being revealed to another person. Our fear of revealing ourselves moves us to create *non*-intimate connection in any form we can get it.

Reclaiming Self is not in fact a wholly pleasurable process. Like any major life change, it can destabilize our existing relationships. Our individuation makes us new and we want to start over, bringing our newness to more promising relationships.

But just walking away from our old, misshapen relationships is an act of Opposition Consciousness, and it fixes nothing. In truth, our existing relationships, as twisted as they seem at times, have the same unlimited potential for newness as *we* have. As reclaimed Selves we reshape every relationship, old or new. With no striving to change other people and no striving to change unsatisfying situations, we create intimacy by *ceasing* to strive—by accepting people and situations just as they are—by being ourselves.

Self-Portrait: Phase Eight

You've been listening to your own voice—asking yourself about your values, indulging your desires—but the layers keep coming. Hours, even days, pass before you realize that you've stopped noticing your use of the language of oppression. Begin again.

Asking yourself what you desire puts the scraper in your hand. Indulging your desire scrapes your canvas clean.

Rest if you like; paint nothing. You decide.

PART FIVE

Reclaiming Self

"One's own self is well hidden from one's own self:
of all mines of treasure, one's own is the last to be dug up."
–Nietzsche

CHAPTER TEN

Reclaiming Self

Reclaiming Self means bringing the *Self* into consciousness.

Each time the voice of Other triggers your self-referential question, "What do I desire?" you take the opportunity to reconnect with your-*self*. When you *desire*, when you *decide* based on your desires, and when you *act* on your decisions, you reclaim Self.

A Three-Step Program

The road to reclaiming Self is three steps long.

Step One: Stop taking guidance from the voice of Other.

It is through your recognition and elimination of the voice of Other that you develop your Self-focus. Self-focus makes you realize that you are responsible for all of your thoughts, words, and actions all the time.

Step Two: Stop *being* the voice of Other.

The more you decline to *be* the voice of Other, the better you hear the voice of Self. When you cease to be the voice of Other, you realize that you are not responsible for anyone else's thoughts, words, or actions. Ever.

Step Three: Refer to yourself with reverence.

Listen for your references to yourself. Do they imply suspicion of your desires, motives, or intentions? Do they sneer at the notion of your self-improvement? Do they imply a desire to limit you in any way? Notice your relationship with the notion of Self, and resolve to speak (and think) of yourself with reverence.

Self-Focus

The three-step program for reclaiming Self clears away the obstacle of Other-focus. It helps you to stop worrying about what others would have you do or be—as well as what's right for other people. When your Other-focus is gone, you are left with Self-focus.

Self-focus is a term that may strike you (if you still harbor suspicion of the Self) as narcissistic. If you still hear with contempt terms like self-importance and self-concern, you may be tempted to plop Self-focus onto the same contemptible heap. But in your quest to de-fang your notion of Self, suspend your suspicion of all of these terms and open yourself to all of the Self's possibilities.

To better understand Self-focus we'll first define its opposite. In Other-focus our satisfaction depends upon either the extent to which others are behaving as we wish they would, or the extent to which we are pleasing others with our behavior. As it is impossible to make others behave at all times as we wish, and it is impossible to know for certain how we might best please others, satisfaction for the Other-focussed person is impossible.

The Other-focussed person has a skewed view of what he or she is personally responsible for. If in our Other-focus we tend to seek guidance, we may believe that we are not personally responsible for our actions, as we so often do what others advise. If in our Other-focus we seek to *guide* other people, we may believe that we are personally responsible for everything and everybody all the time.

The guidance seeker finds protection in her Other-focus. As she does not act on her own desires, she believes she puts Other, rather than herself, up for assessment. If her actions produce unfavorable results, she has someone else to blame. In a short time she finds herself in a cycle in which her Other-focus helps her avoid personal

responsibility and her habit of avoiding personal responsibility increases her Other-focus.

The person who believes he is responsible for everything and everybody may end up even more deeply mired in Other-focus, as the hyper-responsible guide often gets encouragement from others to continue his pattern of care-taking. If someone else is in *need*, he's there with a shoulder, some wisdom, or an answer. He believes that his Other-focus serves an important purpose, and others are quick to affirm his belief. He too finds himself returning again and again to Other-focus, and he has countless people thanking him for it.

We are in each moment either Other-focussed or Self-focussed— there is no in-between. By its contrast to the futility of Other-focus, Self-focus is already an attractive option. But Self-focus has much more to recommend it than its relief from the tyranny of Other-focus.

Self-focus provides us with a set point from which to navigate. Since the Self-focussed individual refers to her*self* in every situation, she finds answers within. She sees challenges as opportunities to review her values; she decides and acts based upon what she desires to do. Because she creates personal solutions to her personal challenges (as opposed to pulling ethical answers out of the ether) she has the ability to figure out what to do. And because she meets personal challenges with personal solutions, her solutions satisfy her personally.

The Self-focussed individual is capable of intimate connection. Free from the obstacles of Other-focus, he creates the opportunity for honest exchange of thoughts, feelings, and ideas. Our focus—Self or Other—determines how we talk, how we listen, and how we receive and respond to others. The Self-focussed individual is not personally threatened by other people, so he remains detached enough to be objective with them. The Self-focussed individual shares himself without dissolving into others, freeing himself and others from the burden of his dissolution. He shares himself without directing others, freeing others from the burden of his assessments (and freeing himself from the burden of monitoring the behavior of others.) And because he experiences his competence through his self-reliance, he feels adequate to reveal himself authentically to others.

Practice

Like liberty and responsibility, Self-focus is a practice—not a condition. And as with all practices, *trying* to master the practice doesn't help. Mastery comes from *practicing* the practice.

Assume your own Self-focus, and practice accordingly. Notice your forays into Other-focus and reclaim your Self-focus with self-referential questioning. Even when you understand and consistently practice Self-focus, moments of Other-focus will come creeping back. You may still occasionally think, "What *should* I do?" or even, "What would my parents do?" These are not moments of failure. Each realization that you've slipped into Other-focus is an opportunity to ask yourself about your desires—an opportunity to view the current situation against the backdrop of your own values.

Kindness

It may seem that Other-focus would serve you better than Self-focus when it comes to treating others kindly. In practice your Other-focus does lead you to concern yourself with how you will be received by others. The Other-focussed person is likely to play out scenes in her head, and might even practice what she will say in order to spare someone's feelings or lead him down the *right* path. She has admirable intentions, but while an isolated incident of well-intentioned Other-focus may seem harmless, it opens us to further Other-focus with its futile speculation about the unknowable.

When you are faced with a decision about what to say to another person, you can either operate from Other-focus and speculate about how you will best be received, or you can embrace your Self-focus and decide how you wish to represent yourself. Other-focus leads you to ask yourself, "How will she take what I want to say to her?" Self-focus leads you to ask, "How can I compassionately convey my position on this issue?"

This second, more personal stance—one based not on your ability to discern what others want, but on your trust in your own personally held value of kindness—is far better "protection" against hurting others. If you operate with others as your focus, always *trying* to determine how you can please them, your foundation will only be as solid as your always-flawed perception of what other people want. If you operate with Self as focus, your foundation is as solid and accessible as your own values.

Peers

Self-focus makes peer relationships possible.

When two people connect, the relationship they build uses both individuals as its foundation. When we undermine our personal foundation with Other-focus, we undermine the foundation of our relationships as well. This implies (an implication that seems rather illogical upon first consideration) that the most valuable action you can take in support of your peer relationships is to maintain your Self-focus.

Compassionate action, honest communication, and giving and receiving love are all supported by Self-focus. Purely ethical action, deep talk that merely mimics intimate communication, and the practice of fearing and deflecting love (no matter what appearance we give to the contrary) are all fed by Other-focus.

Just as important as the assumption of your *own* Self-focus, is your acceptance of others. Even if the people in your life are relentlessly Other-focussed, it does you no good to concern yourself with their focus. (Any speculation about the level to which anyone else is Self- or Other-focussed, is of course an act of your own Other-focus.) It is never a function of Self-focus to wonder about whether another person is experiencing a relationship as an equally balanced peer relationship. If one of you is feeling, thinking, and behaving as a peer, your Self-focus does more to promote peer-ness than any amount of Other-focussed relationship-assessing you could ever do.

Romance

Longevity in healthy intimate relationships depends upon the endurance of attraction. Because attraction ignites Self-to-Self, attraction is nurtured by Self-focus and is eroded quite devastatingly by Other-focus. Our expectation that others will be as we want them to be—or that they will be as we thought they once were—are perils of Other-focus. In Other-focus, your satisfaction depends upon your favorable judgement of the qualities and actions of others.

But our lack of attraction to the object of our fading affection is only part of the peril of our Other-focus. Our own lack of Self-focus can provide less Self for our mate to be attracted to. When you retreat into Other-focus you make yourself unavailable, hiding yourself in worry about Other. You distance from yourself when you dissolve into others, encouraging others to distance from you. They conclude, "If she's not willing to be with herself, why would *I* want to be with her?" The more consistently you maintain Self-focus, the closer you are to being the Self that your mate was attracted to in the first place.

Children

Not all relationships are meant to be peer relationships. Most notably, parents and teachers do not have pure peer relationships with children. It can be challenging to maintain Self-focus while putting a fair amount of emotional energy into the very direct care of other people.

It is a common misconception that small children are the center of their universe. They certainly take a me-first stance at times, but small children are almost entirely Other-focussed. They put forth *needs*, seek validation, make concessions, and take on the emotions of others. Directly following their most independent acts, they look around to see who is watching.

You can begin teaching Self-focus to children when they are still very young, first by your own example. When children become old enough to learn from deliberate teaching, you can teach them how to access their own emotions and to ask themselves about their own values and desires. You can ask them whether it feels better to apologize than it does to sit in a snit, and whether it feels better to cooperate than it does to be disruptive. You can ask them how it feels to hurt someone and then turn away, compared to how it feels to apologize. You can point children toward their emotions and teach them how to collect their own data.

Children are smart, and they have much less contempt for the Self than adults have. If we teach them Self-focus, we'll reap the benefit of that Self-focus as our children become our peers.

Challenging People

The relationships we form before we reclaim ourselves are often marred by imbalances. We may find ourselves in relationships with people who do not behave as peers.

You may wish, as you reclaim Self, to rid yourself of old relationships. Proceed with caution. Even if a relationship appears too imbalanced to salvage, have faith in the muscle of your own Self-focus to reshape it.

When you bring your new Self-focus to your old relationships, those relationships change because you have. You change how you listen and respond to others. While you might previously have reacted to difficult people with sarcasm, criticism, contempt, or (perhaps most damaging of all) advice, your Self-focus allows you to provide a more detached, non-invasive voice for others. When it is no longer your desire to tell people what they *need*, you become far more skilled at asking them what they desire. And when changing others is no longer your goal—perhaps *because* changing others is no longer your goal—others change.

Employ patience, love, empathy, compassion, and consideration in these relationships. (You formed them for a reason.) If you desire it, use distance to create space for change. Give the overly dependent person some room to find someone else to ask what he *should* do. Give the oppressive guide a chance to fix someone else. Upon re-approach, after you have had more time in Self-focus, you will bring a fresher Self to your challenging relationships and you will experience satisfying improvements in them.

Self-focus provides you with a personal sense of security in any relationship. Through consistently referring to yourself—through asking yourself about your desires and using your values to determine your course of action—you gain a clearer perception of who you are. As you see that your values and desires serve you well, you experience the security that comes from trusting yourself.

Self-Portrait: Phase Nine

Look at your self-portrait in its current condition. You've put on thick, muddy layers by accident, scraped them off, applied other layers deliberately and scraped them off as well.

Do you think your best friend would like your self-portrait at this point? What would your neighbors think of it? How about your junior high gym teacher? These are the fretful speculations of Other-focus.

Could you bring your self-portrait into a gallery filled with everyone you've ever known—for all to regard in any way they choose—and not worry about what anyone thought of it? That's Self-focus.

CHAPTER ELEVEN

Something to Do

I went to a bookstore several months ago and asked for recommendations for books about "the Self." The bookseller asked me, "Do you mean the upper-case Self or the lower-case self?" While I had a fairly good grasp of the difference, I wasn't exactly sure which one I was looking for.

Throughout this book I have distinguished the philosophical notion of the Self with a capital "S" and the more practical, everyday notion of the self with the lower-case. But what I've learned since that day in the bookstore is that, in practice, Self and self are one and the same.

The Self is not illusive, Romantic, or heroic; the Self is just the self. As you apply the concepts in this book, you will probably expand your philosophical sense of Self. But more importantly, you will increase your practical grasp on what you might *do* with your *self*. Eliminating the language of oppression—words and phrases that create obligation, frustration, and restriction—will give you that practical grasp.

If you desire to eliminate the language of oppression from your vocabulary, the 40-day program in this chapter will help. Each day you will have an exercise or an inspiration to keep your focus on this task.

Bring a forgiving heart to this endeavor. Each time you catch yourself using one of these oppressive words or phrases is not an opportunity to feel like a failure. Instead, look at each instance as an opportunity to deliberately experience a greater sense of personal freedom. Decide to enjoy each moment you spend experiencing what it feels like to stop and ask yourself, "What do I really want to do?" or to realize, "No, it's not that I *have to* go home—right now I'd *love* to go home."

Eliminating oppressive speech from your vocabulary will create a shift in you. You will find over time that you see yourself as more free and peaceful. The more free and peaceful we all are, the happier, healthier, and more secure our planet is.

Words and Phrases to Notice:

should	have to	must	ought to
should	have to	must	ought to
shouldn't	had to	mustn't	oughtn't
should not	has to	must not	ought not
should have	have go to	must've	ought to have
should've	has got to	must have	ought not have
shouldn't have	gotta	must not have	oughtta
should not have		mustn't have	

try	need	can't	have no choice
try	need	can't	have no choice
trying	needs	cannot	had no choice
tried	needed		has no choice

Day 1: Each time you catch yourself saying *I should*, ask yourself what you desire. Follow your self-referential questions to a satisfying conclusion.

Day 2: Write three sentences that start with *I should*. Think of a desire associated with each idea. Rewrite each sentence in a way that reflects your desire.

1. _____

2. _____

3. _____

1. _____

2. _____

3. _____

Don't let a *should* stand between you and what you want.

Day 3: What people in your life have been *should*-sayers? Forgive them. Again and again.

Day 4: The next time you see a rack of magazines, scan the copy on the covers looking for the language of oppression. Notice how that language makes you feel.

Day 5: Write three sentences that begin with *I can't*. Are they true? Even if they *are*, how might you restate them without affirming self-restriction?

1. _____

2. _____

3. _____

1. _____

2. _____

3. _____

Don't let *I can't* determine the course of your actions.

Day 6: The next time you catch yourself saying you *have no choice*, think of two additional choices—even if they aren't very appealing choices. Choose.

Day 7: Say *I must* to yourself three times. Experience what *I must* feels like in your body. Avoid that feeling in the future.

Day 8: Be tolerant of the use of oppressive speech on TV and in movies. It is everywhere in our society.

Day 9: Write three sentences that start with *I need*. Ask yourself if you really *need* those things or if they are merely desires. Whatever

your answer is, rewrite the sentences repositioning each supposed *need* as a desire.

1. _____

2. _____

3. _____

1. _____

2. _____

3. _____

Learn to reposition *needs* as desires automatically.

Day 10: Rewrite these exclamations using non-oppressive language: *I
have to* get this CD! *I have to* buy these shoes! *I have to* stop
spending so much money!

1. _____

2. _____

3. _____

Invent new ways of expressing enthusiasm.

Day 11: Enjoy catching yourself using the words and phrases on the
elimination list. Each time you catch yourself, see it as an
opportunity to stop and savor your reclamation of Self.

Day 12: Be compassionate when other people use the language of
oppression. Accept it just as it is.

Day 13: Write a note to someone you love. It can be about anything;
just be sure to avoid using *should, have to, must, ought to, try,
need, can't* and *have no choice* in your note. Seal it, bless it, and
send it.

Day 14: Discuss the elimination of oppressive speech with a friend or
family member. Feel free to copy this chapter and share it with
others.

Day 15: When you feel a sense of obligation toward someone you love, don't act from the obligation, act from the love.

Day 16: Write a sentence that includes the word *try*, where *try* means "to test." (Only the use of *try* that means "to strive" is oppressive.)

_____

_____

Decide which uses of *try* you wish to replace.

Day 17: List five daily activities that sometimes feel like obligations.

1. _____

2. _____

3. _____

4. _____

5. _____

How many of these activities are things you don't mind doing? How many of them do you actually enjoy doing? How many of them will you stop doing?

Day 18: Say out loud, *"I'm trying, I'm trying, I'm trying."* Experience how *trying* feels in your body. Avoid that feeling in the future.

Day 19: Contemplate the value you place on *"trying* really hard." Do you place an inordinately high value on effort? Create a belief about *"trying* really hard" that reflects your current values.

Day 20: Listen to children talking. Listen for words that convey obligation, frustration, and restriction. How does the language of oppression make you feel when it's voiced by children?

Day 21: Think of someone you love very much, but whom you haven't spoken to in years. Forgive yourself for having lost touch. Call that person, and have a conversation using only non-oppressive language.

Day 22: All language is creative. Give a compliment today and notice what you create.

Day 23: Reshape these sentences using non-oppressive language: Do you *need* directions? We *need* a plan. I *have to* leave by noon.

1. _____

2. _____

3. _____

These aren't easy. That's why we practice.

Day 24: Have you noticed any improvement in your overall mood since you began eliminating oppressive speech from your vocabulary?

Day 25: Set a boundary today. Ask for what you want in a loving and respectful way. How does that boundary represents you?

Day 26: Come up with uses for the word *should* that do not convey obligation. (There are only a few.) Notice when you use them in conversation and decide whether you should like to keep using them or find alternatives.

Day 27: Consider taking up an old talent or endeavor—something that you once loved to do but stopped.

Day 28: Notice that you will sometimes talk with people who are completely unwilling to give up feelings of oppression. Retain your Self-focus. You are not responsible for anyone else's experience.

Day 29: Think of one thing you can do that you are not doing already that would increase your sense of personal integrity. Decide whether you want to do it.

Day 30: Notice the difference between how it feels to say *I have to* and how it feels to say *I don't have to*. You may find that *I don't have to* has a defensiveness in it that doesn't feel any better than the obligation of *I have to*. What other language might you use to express a freedom from obligation?

Day 31: Think of one thing that you still feel is an obligation. Consider it from another angle and choose not to see it as an obligation. What remains when the sense of obligation is removed?

Day 32: Draw or paint a picture; write a story or poem. Keep it for only as long as you appreciate it.

Day 33: The next time you have a difference of opinion with someone, retain your Self-focus. You are not responsible for anyone else's values, beliefs, ideas, or priorities.

Day 34: Is there anyone in your life with whom you have an uncomfortable relationship? Have you been feeling like you don't know how to improve that relationship? Deep down, you do.

Day 35: Recall a time when someone asked too much of you. How might you assert your desires and retain your Self-focus in a similar situation?

Day 36: What are your plans for today? What do you wish your plans were for today? Amend your plans at least slightly to reflect your desires.

Day 37: Think about the people you feel closest to. Are they "high energy?" "serene and peaceful?" "stressed out?" Contemplate how Self-focus helps you to be in relationship with a variety of people without letting them determine your mood.

Day 38: Which of your talents do you value most? Find an opportunity to use it today.

Day 39: What do you love to create? Create it today.

Day 40: Do you feel more free and peaceful and powerful than you did on Day One? If you do, then you are.

Self-Portrait: Phase Ten

You have unbreakable brushes, a lifetime supply of paint, and most importantly, a scraper you know how to use. You have the ability to repaint yourself in any way you choose, as many times as you please. You have the tools to scrape away your layers of identity and to reveal your purest, least affected Self.

You are on your way to a richer understanding of who you are. And you have the rest of your life to figure out what to do about it.

Acknowledgments

It is with love and appreciation that I acknowledge all who have helped in the creation of this book. I will mention a mere 38 of them by name.

Ester Gorsky knew I had a book in me the minute she met me. She made abstract for me what had always been concrete. **Pat Kaluza** taught me about being self-referential and that a destiny to be self-indulgent was what the Universe wanted from me. She made concrete for me what had always been abstract. **Elleva Joy McDonald** took me to visit my Self through her work as an **Avatar®** Master. The Avatar tools bring joy and healing to everyone they touch. **Carolyn Brunner** taught me acceptance and so much more. **Cara Beams** taught me self-differentiation. **Harriet Lerner's** *The Dance of Intimacy* taught me Self-focus. **Alice Miller** taught me that if it happened, it happened. **Dr. Robert Bitzer** taught me "the thing itself." **Michelle Mooney, Dominic LaBella, Virginia Campbell, Tracine Asberry, Stephen Anunson, Anthoney Green, Becky Russie, Jill Hanson, Alexis Walsko, Carolyn Walsko, Barb Nault, Jenny Sponberg, Aaron Murphy, Janet Feldman, Mary Jo Rieger, Val Olson, Dana Smith, Manuel Amunategui,** and **Dave Smith** read my roughs and told the truth. **Marilyn Pash** said, "*Shoulds* and *oughts* and *can'ts.*" **Lori Stellman** said, "Yes, you *do* know what you want." **Norman Heinitz** said, "I know you can do it." **MaryAnn Heinitz** said, "Let them see the sparkle." **Nigel Naughton** put my wheels back on. **Jerene Carlson** saw the finished product a year before it was written. **Cal Appleby** took me to my audience. **Jean Keating** handed me a scraper. **Philipp Goedicke** saved me a hundred times. **Ella Smith** is my inspiration. **Darin Smith** stood by me from start to finish—enduring much along the way.

*Avatar is a registered trademark of Star's Edge International.

About the Author

Rebecca Smith has worked as an Engli[sh] ...[tea]cher in Milwaukee and a wardrobe consultant in Minneap[olis] ...time author, she is qui- etly building a reputation as an ...[wri]ting, and compelling speaker.

She lives in Min... ...na named Ella.

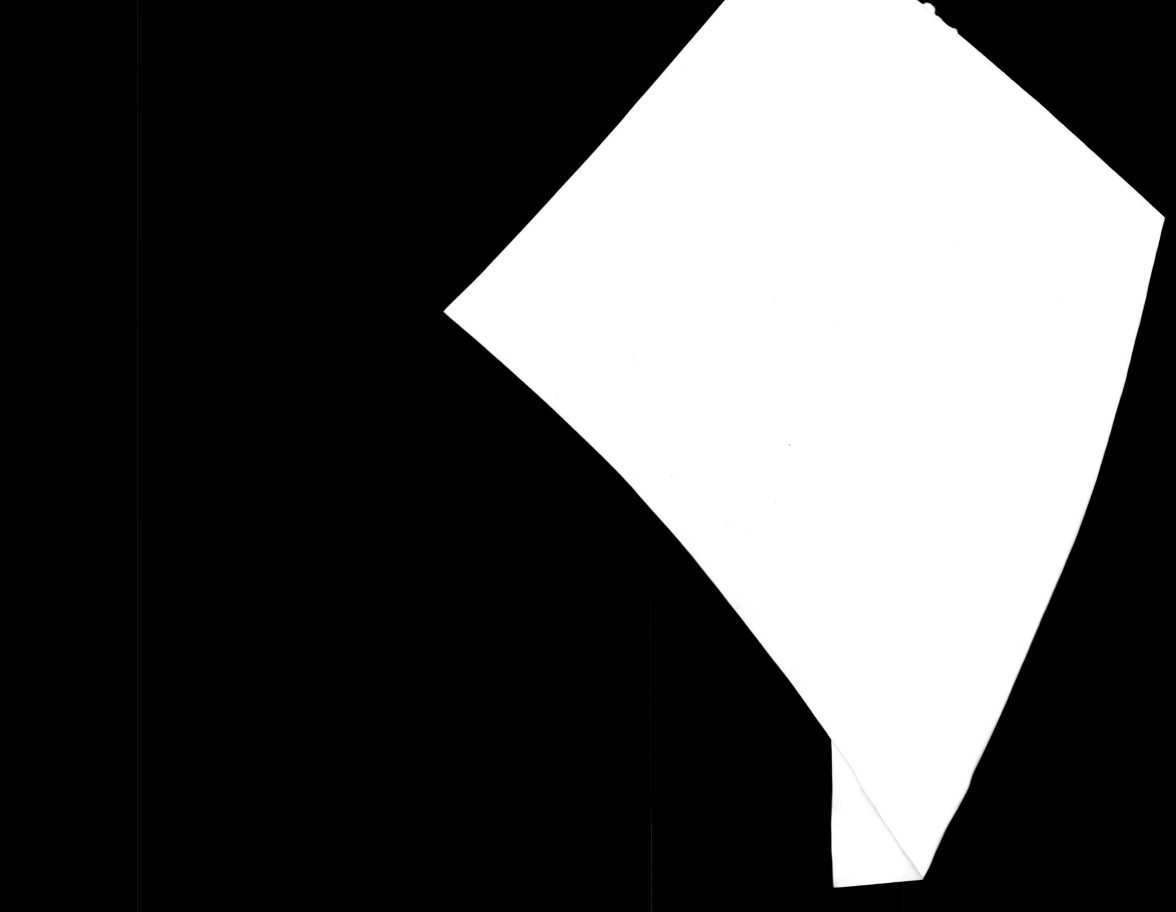